THE RE... (......)

Volume 28

Volume 26

Volume 24

Volume 23

Volume 22

Volume 20

THE REFERENCE SHELF

Vol. 32   No. 3

OUTLOOK

FOR THE

RAILROADS

Edited by
POYNTZ TYLER

THE H. W. WILSON COMPANY
NEW YORK   1960

PREFACE

The United States has been called, among other things, "an experiment in transportation." It is an apt description, for the history of the United States is the history of a mobile people marching across a continent and leaving in its wake the most efficient industrial and agricultural economy upon earth. That march and the development that followed were made possible by the almost simultaneous construction of a unique, effective, and nation-wide system of transportation and to gauge the effect of this system upon the North American continent one need only look at the others. South America, Asia, and Africa—all blessed with equal or greater natural resources—have been developed only around the edges, in regions close to the sea. Their great interior resources remain largely untouched because they lack the transportation facilities that have made the United States and southern Canada a modern miracle of production, manufacture, communication, and trade.

Even in our own short history it is a recent miracle, for our colonial ancestors had little need of inland transportation. Huddled along the coast, they could trade with one another over the great tidal rivers, trade with the world over the very sea that had brought them here. Only when they went "over the mountains" into the great central areas and on to the Pacific did they feel the need for transport by land, and to meet that need they fashioned the complex system of communication that we have inherited. First they built the roads, the rough roads that often followed Indian trails and were of more social than economic worth until the internal combustion engine made them into the great webs of concrete we know today. Then they built canals to supplement the natural waterways that had served their fathers. And finally they built the railroads.

It is the railroads that are the subject of this book—the railroads that form such an important part of the great system of roads, rails, pipelines, inland waterways, and airways that constitute the American system of interior transportation. Their history is one of strife and turmoil, of bravery and dedication and will, and their history can only be touched upon here. It is too long and too vital to be compressed within the covers of a single book, just as their future is too clouded with uncertainty and doubt to make it dependent upon one economic factor or upon one course of action. Today there is only one certainty about the future of the railroads and that certainty is that the railroads are here to stay. The laws of physics and gravity have combined to make the flanged wheel on a steel track the most versatile and efficient means of interior transport ever devised and the continued operation of those laws will keep the wheels turning and the tracks in use. What power will drive the wheels, what power or powers will govern the tracks, only the coming years can decide, but by peering into the past and examining the present the writers of this book have been able to give us a glimpse of what the future might hold. To these writers and to their publishers the editor is deeply grateful for permission to use their work.

POYNTZ TYLER

April 1960

For an examination of other aspects of the American transportation system, the reader should consult *Airways of America* (Volume 30, Number 6 of The Reference Shelf) and *American Highways Today* (Volume 29, Number 1).

CONTENTS

I. THE IRON HORSE

EDITOR'S INTRODUCTION

Back in 1807, when the cabinet of President Thomas Jefferson was pondering how the great continental area of the new Federal Union might be brought and held together, Secretary of the Treasury Albert Gallatin sought the advice of eminent men in many fields. One of his advisors was Robert Fulton, whose *Clermont* had steamed up the Hudson River that very year, another was Benjamin H. Latrobe, engineer and architect of the Capitol at Washington, and each man replied in his own image. The internal communications of America, said Mr. Fulton, could best be served by a system of canals—canals that ranged from waterways of commerce to small lateral ditches two or three feet deep to accommodate local traffic and local freight. Mr. Latrobe, although conceding the advantages of canals, recommended "artificial roads." By artificial roads he meant turnpikes, but in a brief postscript he mentioned and dismissed a new sort of artificial road lately introduced into England. "The astonishing loads drawn upon rail roads by single horses in England have induced many of our citizens to hope for their early application to the use of our country," he wrote, "but I fear this hope is vain excepting on a very limited scale" since the cost of the "erection of a rail road" could be justified only by "a very great demand for its use." Such a demand Latrobe could not foresee, except possibly in the limited field of carrying heavy minerals for short distances. The "carriage of common articles" by rail road was "out of the question."

Latrobe was describing the horse-drawn colliery lines of England (the first English railroad was built to carry coals to Newcastle) and his views of the railroad were the views of his time. Both his views and his time were short-lived. Within a few years his own son was to become chief engineer for the Baltimore & Ohio Railroad, built to connect the Atlantic seaboard with the Mississippi Valley, and before this first "long-distance line" in the world had reached its western terminus the railroad fever that is described in this section was already on the rise. By the time Latrobe's son died in 1875 the Federal Union he had advised tying together with "artificial roads" was being bound together with bands of steel.

The articles which follow in this section give a composite picture of the development of American railroads from the earliest days down to the present age of Diesels. Although mechanical improvements are discussed (in "Up from the Wood Burners"), the chief emphasis is on the enormous and continuing importance of railroads in our social and economic life.

THE GREAT IRON SKEIN [1]

Of all the forms of transportation which have been developed during man's onward march, the one which has contributed most to the spread of civilization, the creation and diffusion of wealth, the expansion of industries, and improvements in the standard of living, is the railroad. No other industry so fully enters into the everyday life of the American people.

To realize how true this is we have only to consider the important part which railway transportation plays in assembling the materials which go into the production of our homes, the furniture and furnishings with which our homes are fitted, the food we eat, the clothing we wear, and the many other things we use and see about us.

Many of these articles have been brought to us by rail—sometimes for thousands of miles—and if we should trace them back still further, we would find that railway transportation played an important part in assembling the raw materials from which most of them were made. So we see there is a close relationship between railway transportation and the comforts and advantages which we enjoy every hour of the day.

Moreover, railroads have been tremendously important from the broader standpoint of national development. Until the advent

[1] From booklet, *American Railroads, Their Growth and Development.* Association of American Railroads. Transportation Building. Washington 6, D.C. '58. p 3-20. Reprinted by permission.

of railroads, the nation's inland commerce moved principally upon canals, lakes and navigable rivers when ice, low water or floods did not interfere.

On land, people were dependent upon the stagecoach for long journeys, and the Conestoga wagon for freight haulage. Travel and communication were slow, and the cost of transporting freight long distances by land was often prohibitive. Lack of efficient land transportation retarded agricultural and industrial development and confined trade to small areas.

As railroads spread across the nation, vast changes occurred. In many parts of the country railroads were the pioneers, opening immense regions to farming, mining, lumbering and manufacturing. In older parts of the country, with the coming of the railroads, communities took on new life and a new outlook. Wherever the rails were laid down, towns sprang into being, industry took root, commerce developed, communication was speeded up, agricultural production increased, and land values were multiplied. Distance no longer was a barrier to trade. Railroads founded and developed new markets for producers, new sources of supply for consumers.

When the first common carrier railroads were opened, in 1830, there were less than 13 million people in the United States —nearly all located in the area east of the Mississippi River. In the entire region west of the Mississippi River, including the Pacific Coast area, there were fewer people than there are today in the city of Richmond, Virginia. In the entire country, there were then only five cities of more than 25,000 inhabitants—New York, Philadelphia, Baltimore, Boston, and New Orleans—all located on or near the seacoasts. Today, there are about five hundred cities with populations ranging from 25,000 upward, and they are distributed throughout the country. Industrial and agricultural growth has been equally striking.

Of course, it would be absurd to suggest that the railroads alone have brought this country to its present state of development. Many factors have contributed to the nation's growth and progress, but students of American history agree that the railroads have played a major role in the building of our nation.

Why, one may ask, has the railroads' contribution to economic progress been greater than that of other agencies of transportation? The answer is that railroads go everywhere, they carry everything, and they perform their transportation service without interruption at all seasons of the year. They handle bulk freight, package freight, perishable freight, passengers, and mail. Their service can be made to fit every transportation need. It is speedy, cheap, and more dependable than that of any other mode of transportation.

Then, too, railroads are great industries in themseles. Wherever the railroads go, they become large local investors, and they become important local taxpayers. They build and maintain station buildings, repair shops, yards, and supply depots. They provide regular employment to local workers.

Moreover, railroads assure communities, cities, and industries more permanent transportation service than does any other agency. When a railroad enters a community, it casts its lot with that community through thick and thin, at all seasons, year in and year out. It is this assurance of dependable all-year-round transportation that makes for permanent community growth and prosperity.

Beginnings of Railway Development

The first locomotive to run on rails in the United States—or in the New World for that matter—was a small experimental engine built by Colonel John Stevens and operated on a circular railway track at Hoboken, New Jersey, in 1825. It was never put to practical use.

The first locomotive to run on a standard railroad in the United States was the British-built *Stourbridge Lion.* On August 8, 1829, the *Lion,* operated by Horatio Allen, a young civil engineer, was tried out on a short, wooden railroad in Pennsylvania.

In September of that year, the *Tom Thumb,* an experimental locomotive built by Peter Cooper of New York, was given a trial run on a newly-built railroad at Baltimore, Maryland. This little engine, weighing about one ton, was the first American-built locomotive to run on a common carrier railroad in this country.

Meanwhile, the pioneer railroad of the South was getting under way at Charleston, South Carolina. In December 1830, scheduled steam passenger service—the first in America—was introduced on that road.

The first train was powered by the 3½-ton locomotive *Best Friend of Charleston,* built at the West Point Foundry, New York City, and shipped to Charleston by sailing vessel. The *Best Friend* was the first locomotive to pull a train of cars on an American railroad.

The opening of the first railroads in Maryland and South Carolina in 1830 marked the real beginning of the railway era in America. These railroads, although beset by many perplexing problems, demonstrated the superiority of railroads over other forms of transportation and brought forward-looking citizens to a realization that here was a mode of transportation which had immense possibilities because of its comparative cheapness, its adaptability to the many needs of trade and commerce, its promise of speed, and its ability to provide all-year-round service.

By 1835 more than two hundred railway charters had been granted in eleven states and more than a thousand miles of railroad had been opened for operation. Only a few of the many early companies succeeded in actually building railroads, and still fewer companies survived for any considerable length of time. However, railroads were built in Ohio, Michigan, Indiana, Kentucky, Tennessee, Alabama, Mississippi and Louisiana, as well as in states bordering the Atlantic Ocean. In some instances these small railroads of the 1830's formed the nuclei for, or later became parts of, the important railway systems of today.

By 1850, there were more than nine thousand miles of railroad in the United States. The railroads of that day were short, but many of them were connected with other lines to form through routes of travel and commerce. For instance, in 1850 one could travel by rail all the way from Waterville, Maine, to Buffalo, New York, by using some twelve different railroads and changing cars several times en route. Such a journey required about four days—considerably more time than is now required to travel by train from coast to coast.

Federal Land Grants to Pioneer Railroads

For many years the Federal Government followed a policy of encouraging the development of highways and canals through the public domain by granting sections of land along the proposed routes to help defray the cost of construction. In 1850, Congress passed the first land-grant measure to aid in the construction of railroads. The specific purpose of the act was to promote the construction of a through rail route from the Great Lakes to the Gulf of Mexico.

This congressional land grant to Illinois, Mississippi and Alabama consisted of alternate even-numbered sections for six miles on either side of the proposed rail routes. The government had offered these lands for many years at $1.25 an acre, but there were no buyers because of the lack of transportation.

When the land-grant act was passed, the government immediately advanced the price of the acreage which it retained in the land-grant strips to $2.50 an acre, or double the former price, and, with a railroad assured, the lands were eagerly snapped up by settlers. Thus, the government lost nothing by this exchange of values; on the contrary, it actually gained because the alternate odd-numbered sections retained in each land-grant strip sold for as much as the government had asked, but had been unable to obtain, for the entire strip before the railroad was projected.

From 1850 to 1871, the Federal Government continued its policy of granting lands to aid in the construction of pioneer railroads through sparsely-settled or unsettled areas of the public domain. This method proved highly successful to both the Federal and state governments and the country at large. The land-grant policy gave impetus to the construction of several strategically important railway lines, and these lines contributed greatly to western development.

The railroads created a market for hundreds of millions of acres of public lands which previously had been unsalable at any price because of lack of transportation; they created billions of dollars of new wealth; they enhanced the value of both publicly- and privately-owned lands; they converted non-taxable areas into taxable properties, and they accelerated agricultural and industrial development. The extension of railway transportation to the Pacific Coast region united and solidified the nation at a critical period in its history.

Of the total railway mileage in the United States today, about 8 per cent received Federal grants of land as an aid to construction. Contrary to a popular impression, the land grants were not *gifts* to the railroads. In return for the grants, the railroads for many years carried government troops and property at one-half of standard rates and United States mails for four fifths of established rates. Congress repealed the mail and nonmilitary government traffic provisions in 1941 and the military traffic rates in 1946.

Before their repeal, however, these rate deductions repaid the government many times over for the lands granted. The 131 million acres of land-grant lands which the railroads received from the Federal Government were valued at slightly less than one dollar an acre, or a total of about $125 million, at the time they were granted. In March 1945, the Interstate Commerce Committee of the House of Representatives reported that the railroads had already "contributed over $900 million in payment of the lands which were transferred to them under the Land Grant Acts." Between the time of that report and the end of land-grant deductions in government rates, there were further payments estimated at not less than $350 million. Thus, the total contributions of the railroads to the government through rate deductions on account of land grants were approximately ten times the value of the lands at the time they were granted to the railroads.

Rails to the Pacific

As late as 1850 there was not a mile of railroad west of the Mississippi River. But the discovery of gold in California, the lure of trans-Pacific trade, and the land-grant policy of the Federal Government were giving impetus to westward railway expansion.

The first railroad to be opened west of the Mississippi River was commenced at St. Louis, Missouri, in 1851. The first locomotive on that pioneer road was the *Pacific,* sometimes called *Pacific No. 3,* which arrived at St. Louis from the East in August, 1852, and made its initial run a few miles out of St. Louis on December 1 of that year.

During the 1850's several railroads were built westward from the Mississippi, and by 1860 the "Iron Horse" was on the Missouri.

Between 1850 and 1860 railway mileage in the United States increased from 9,021 to 30,626 miles. The country was growing by leaps and bounds, with the railroads playing a major role. Many railroads were under construction; numerous others were contemplated. One of these was the road across the Great Plains and through the western mountains to the Pacific Coast— a line two and one half times longer than the longest railroad then existing in the world.

In 1863, President Abraham Lincoln fixed the eastern terminus of the proposed transcontinental railroad at Omaha, Nebraska Territory. In California, a company was organized to build a railroad eastward from Sacramento to meet the road from Omaha. Ground was broken at Omaha and Sacramento in 1863, and construction was pushed with vigor. Tracklaying progressed with amazing speed. Boom towns mushroomed along the right-of-way as the tracks advanced. Swarms of land-hungry settlers followed in the wake of the rails. Finally, on May 10, 1869, the construction forces met and the rails were joined at Promontory, north of Great Salt Lake. A train from the East and a train from the West approached and halted within a few feet of each other. Then, between the noses of the two locomotives, a memorable scene was enacted. The symbolic golden spike was driven, signalizing the completion of the first chain of railroads to span the American continent. From Utah to points throughout the nation flashed the thrilling telegraph message—"The last rail is laid. The last spike driven. The Pacific Railroad is completed!"

The golden spike marked the completion of the greatest railway project the world had yet seen. It ended the necessity of long voyages around Cape Horn. It brought an end to the journey by ship to the Isthmus of Panama, the trip through the jungle to the Pacific, and then by vessel to California. It also brought an end to the long and perilous overland trip by stagecoach or covered wagon. The railroad united the East and the West—brought the cities of the Atlantic and the Pacific within a few days' journey of each other and opened up a vast and fertile region for settlement and development.

Rails to Everywhere

With the Atlantic and Pacific linked by rail, the conquest of the West was in full swing. During the 1870's and 1880's many other important railway lines were built, opening up large areas of rich territory. In 1881 rails were joined in New Mexico to form the second rail route to the Pacific Coast and the first direct line to southern California. In 1883 a railroad was completed between St. Paul and the Pacific Northwest. In 1888 a southern route between Chicago and California was completed, and in 1893 another great trunk line stretched from the Great Lakes to Puget Sound. Still another route to the Pacific Northwest was completed in 1909, and in 1910 a new rail line was completed from Salt Lake City to San Francisco Bay.

The decade 1880 to 1890 witnessed the most rapid railway expansion in American history. In that ten-year period, 7,030 miles of railroad a year were added—a total increase of 70,300 miles in a single decade. This unparalleled expansion was not confined to the region west of the Mississippi. Railway mileage in Florida more than quadrupled during the ten-year period; that of Mississippi and North Carolina more than doubled; and that of Alabama, Georgia, Kentucky, Michigan, West Virginia and Wisconsin nearly doubled. The expansion of the railway network continued through the 1890's and with diminishing pace up to 1916, by which time every state and nearly every county and every important city and town in the United States was served by one or more railroads and was provided with daily railway service to and from all parts of the country.

In 1916, railway mileage reached its peak—254,000 miles. Since then the aggregate length of road has dropped to about 220,000 miles. However, this does not mean that the railway

plant has been retrogressing since 1916. The contrary is true. . . .
American railway development has been in a constant process
of evolution, tending toward unification, coordination, and consolidation of facilities and services. This trend has been dic-
tated not only by the need for economy, but also by the need for
providing uninterrupted travel and shipping services throughout
the nation, and by the further need for adapting railway services
to the ever-changing transportation demands of a fast-growing
country. Consolidations have resulted in a gradual reduction
in the total number of railway operating companies. In 1911,
the Interstate Commerce Commission reported 1,312 operating
railroads in the United States. At the beginning of 1958, there
were 661 operating railroads, including switching and terminal
companies, or about one half the number in 1911. . . .

Most of the large railway systems of today are the result
of numerous consolidations. Before 1851, for example, eleven
separate and distinct companies owned and operated the railroads composing the line between Albany and Buffalo, New
York. All major systems today are made up of what were once
scores, or even hundreds, of separate and distinct railway
properties.

EARLY DAYS [2]

Railroad Fever

From about 1832 to the end of the century epidemics of a
disease that came to be known as Railroad Fever broke out
sporadically in the United States. A really violent outbreak in
any particular region was almost sure to be followed by a relapse;
and the relapse, in turn, was followed by a condition approaching sanity in which railroads were looked at realistically.

The inception and progress of the fever came in time to have
a pattern. First, some up-and-coming individual, or simply a
fanatical dreamer, said forcibly that what his home town of
Brownsville needed, if it were to share in America's great

[2] From *The Story of American Railroads* by Stewart H. Holbrook, newspaperman
and author of books on American historical subjects. This selection (from p 40-9
and p 3-16) is reprinted by permission of the publishers, Crown Publishers. New
York. '47. Copyright 1947 by Crown Publishers.

destiny, was a steam railroad. He talked the idea to anyone in Brownsville who would listen or could not get away, and the more he talked, because of the very nature of one-idea men, the better the idea seemed to him. It grew and blossomed and burgeoned and even soared, meanwhile taking on all of the beautiful hues of the sky in the Land of Opportunity. It also dripped with gold, gold for all of Brownsville, soon to be a mighty metropolis, teeming with commerce, with industry, with the stir and bustle of countless travelers.

As the virus of the fever began to circulate, it got under the skins of several of Brownsville's leading citizens, almost any one of whom was alert for some new way to turn an honest or at least a respectable dollar. Yes, sir, no matter how you looked at it, the idea did have possibilities. A meeting was held, followed by many more, and if temperature rose to the proper pitch, an application was made to the state for a charter for the Brownsville Rail-Road Corporation.

The legislature debated. And because Americans of the period had invested a total of $250 million in canals and would-be canals, there were stout speeches made against granting the railroad charter by the officers and hired creatures of the canal companies. . . .

But a charter was granted to the would-be railroad men of Brownsville, and to men in hundreds of other places both large and small. So, they sent out surveyors, or at least lookers-at-the-land, who followed up the creeks and rivers, noting the grades, putting a stake here, another there, and finally making a report to the budding corporation: "A line of steam rail-way cars between Brownsville and Columbia City is entirely feasible. . . ." The railroad builders then looked at the maps, saw that Columbia City was twenty miles, or at least eighteen miles, west of Brownsville, and then added ". . . & Western" to the corporate title.

Now began the raising of money, the selling of stock or bonds or both in the projected railroad. Possibly some local practitioner of letters was engaged to write a splendid pamphlet outlining the opportunity offered in the stock of the Brownsville & Western Rail-Road. He could lay it on heavylike, too, for each of the corporation's officers could submit some excellent reason why the road would repay investors manyfold, nor were they men to halter the lively imagination of a gifted composer of beautiful prose.

Usually, too, an orator was called into consultation, for this was a period when sonorous sounds from stump or platform were highly thought of and most effective. In certain towns, so the record shows, the initial sum deemed necessary to start construction was raised within a few days after application of the pamphlet and the oratory to the public pulse. There was simply no resistance; the virus was so active that no real sales efforts were necessary. In other places, however, and these were often communities where money had been raised by selling stock in canals that were never dug, the going was harder, much harder. In which case, reconditioned lightning-rod and patent-medicine salesmen were rushed into the breach. Needy pastors were hurriedly converted to steam, and they presently could see God's hand on the throttle. A newspaper might be purchased, or even started, for the express purpose of boosting the Brownsville & Western. Eminent charlatans and eminent honest men, both were quoted as saying that one share of stock in the new venture, costing a mere $1000, would be worth ten times that amount "in a year's time, mark my words."

Widows and old men and guardians of fools and minors were told how a thousand dollars would not only help to make Brownsville a leading city of the nation, but would also return a multitude of rich dividends, now and forever. Rallies were held, if needed, and resistance broken down by the combined assaults of oratory plus food and drink. And when the laying of the first rail—usually a log with an iron strap along its upper side—was done with great ceremony, and the Hon. Member of Congress let out the *vox humana* stop and poured the wondrous magic of his voice over the assembled citizenry, it was a hard-headed and moody man indeed who could not glimpse the setting sun and the Western ocean at the other end of the Brownsville rails. . . .

By the beginning of 1837 at least two hundred railroads were being operated, built, projected, planned, or merely talked about. Most of them managed to get charters. Millions of dollars changed hands for the paper of stocks and bonds, which were often, and with no regard for their actual worth, things of beauty. A right handsome job were the stock certificates of the New Albany & Salem Rail Road Company of Indiana, crisp rag paper bright with green and gold and carrying also a work of art in a depiction of a New Albany & Salem locomotive and four-car train, smoking around a curve in the Hoosier wildwood. Incidentally, a share of the NA&S (later the Monon) cost $50; and its bonds, not nearly so gaudy, could be had for $10 each. . . .

In spite of all of the enthusiasm, there was also a small yet stiff opposition, and a whole heap of lethargy, about railroads. There were, for instance, many rich men who simply could not bring themselves to the belief that the old order really was changing, that the day of the coach and the canal was done, or swiftly passing. These men had come to manhood and to success without the aid of such things as a steam railroad. Every circumstance of their lives was harnessed to the old ways. Now they were being harassed by a lot of strange new fanatics who waved plans, surveys, and charters, and demanded cash for immediate construction of fantastic roads of rails, on which were to run smoking, stinking, dangerous locomotive monsters.

In Boston, as an instance, Editor Buckingham of the *Courier,* who held himself a progressive man, laid into the idea of a railroad from Boston to Albany with scorn and gusto. Wrote he in his paper:

Alcibiades or some other great man of antiquity, it is said, cut off his dog's tail, that quidnuncs might not become extinct from want of excitement. Some such notion, we doubt not, moved one or two of our experimental philosophers to get up a project of a railroad from Boston to Albany—a project which every one knows, who knows the simplest rule in arithmetic, to be impracticable, but at an expense little less than the market value of the whole territory of Massachusetts; and which, if practicable, every person of common sense knows, would be as useless as a railroad from Boston to the moon.

There was another thing to be considered, too. Were rail-roads moral? Many honest men believed that the railroads would, in some inexplicable manner, have an influence to lower public and private morals. When this question was raised, as it often was in New England, the railroad promotors and builders worked in a purposeful manner on preachers. The Western Railroad of Massachusetts, which became the Boston & Albany and was nowhere near so useless as a railroad from Boston to the moon, ran into the moral issue and to meet it sent a general letter to parsons in the Bay State in which it alleged that "the moral effect of Rail-Roads" was bound to be good and asked, in so many words, that ". . . you take an early opportunity to deliver a Discourse on the Moral effect of Rail-Roads in our wide extended country."

In many regions the struggling railroads actually did need the help of the parsons, and of all other men they could enlist on their side, for the canal, the steamboat, and the stagecoach lines were combining in a savage campaign to stop the progress of the rails. . . .

Yet in spite of organized opposition the . . . fever spread westward rapidly. In 1835 Ohio's first railroad, the Mad River & Lake Erie, was building. In the wilds of Kentucky, Frankfort and Lexington were laying strapiron rails on limestone slabs to connect those towns. The legislature of Indiana granted charters to six projected lines in 1832 alone and nineteen more in the next four years. In Virginia, the Richmond, Fredericksburg & Potomac Railroad Company found the Old Dominion ready to buy some of its stock. Since 1784 it had been the policy of Virginia to encourage transportation by subscribing to the stock of canal, turnpike, and toll-bridge concerns, and now it could see no reason why it should not do the same for the railroads. In 1941 the state of Virginia still retained the 2,752 shares of stock in this pioneer railroad that it had acquired in 1834.

But it was Illinois that decided to go the whole hog, as a state, into the business of both canals and railroads. Early in 1837 the Illinois legislature committed the state, in what must have been a singularly untrammeled meeting, to the creation of more than 1,300 miles of railroad, together with the improvement of many rivers, the digging of several canals, and the construction of many turnpikes. This measure, an omnibus affair cooked up to please everybody in the state and known as the Internal Improvements Bill, provided for the expenditure of $10,250,000 on fifteen projects, in addition to several million dollars already appropriated for construction of the Illinois and Michigan Canal.

In the entire state of Illinois at the time there lived only a few thousand people. There were no cities, and the spaces between villages and farms were immense. Yet the Internal Improvements Bill was passed after noble lobbying by Stephen A. Douglas and other politicians who owned land in the region. One may wonder how the state would have managed to go about carrying out the measure, but the panic of 1837 arrived promptly and put an end to the biggest single railroad dream of the era. Illinois, however, had incurred a huge debt through the fraud and collusion perpetrated by its swindling officials who had, of course, made jobs for themselves as "surveyors," "land buyers," and "estimators." Only a few miles of rail were laid before the panic struck. The state was left crippled with debt, and the consequent high taxes acted to discourage immigration to Illinois for many years. New settlers passed it by for Wisconsin and Iowa.

The panic of 1837 was sudden, devastating, thorough. Food riots broke out during February in New York and other cities. Stores and flour mills and warehouses were raided and looted. Banks refused to honor their own notes. Hard money went into hiding. In attempts to stem the debacle, public men gave utterances to fatuous noises of optimism, and Daniel Webster was sent through the country to announce, in the great voice that held even his enemies spellbound, that the country was fundamentally sound. The ensuing depression lasted a full seven years. It mowed down the current inflation to size by immediately tumbling the fantastic prices of land. And it laid many a budding railroad, or railroad corporation—which were not the same thing—into a grave so deep that their very names are to be found only in old records. One can appreciate the feelings of the treasurer of the Syracuse & Auburn, just before it lost its shirt and its locomotive and its rails, when he wrote: "I am almost in despair. Is there no sale for our stock?" There wasn't, and the company was reduced to issuing IOU notes for bills as low as five dollars. . . .

Though the early part of the 1840's was required to recover from the '37 panic . . . the Federal Government was beginning to take some notice of the new railroads. As early as 1834 it was sending mail in closed pouches by train, and in 1838 Congress passed an act declaring all railroads to be post routes, and the carrying of mail became a regular thing, though the railway postal car was still twenty years in the future. As early as 1840 Amos Kendall, Postmaster General, felt obliged to report on the many delays in mail between New York and Boston. Although this route was composed of steamboat, railroad, and stagecoach carriers, and winds, bad roads, and weather had occasioned several delays, it was snow that had held up the mail on the all-rail Boston-Worcester route—nine serious delays in one season.

For any extended journey the traveler was still obliged to use railroad *and* steamboat, and possibly stagecoach and canal boat as well. Competition between the various modes of transportation, and between the various lines, was savage. As usual in such cases, then as now, a fringe of parasites attached itself to legitimate business. One of the forms parasites took in that era was that of the forwarding house. These employed runners to go after trade and held a contract with a railroad line, or a steamboat, or stagecoach, or perhaps all three, by which the forwarding house bought tickets very cheaply and sold them as dearly as the traffic would bear.

The forwarding houses compounded extortion with fraud. Their runners hung around depots and the taverns that were used as stations, and fastened themselves like leeches on any person who appeared to be going on a journey. To secure a passenger, they talked and shouted and even fought each other, with fists, clubs, even guns. When they had hooked him, and hooked is the word, they sold him what purported to be a ticket, a through ticket, that would carry him, say, from New York to Buffalo without further cost. More often than not the fast-talking runner alleged that the ticket also included all meals along the way, and even lodging at stopovers. The tickets were usually elaborate printing jobs, embellished with pictures of rairoad trains, canal boats, and stagecoaches, all moving with the speed of the wind toward their destination.

But many a victim of the runners discovered on his arrival at Albany that the runner's ticket actually took him only as far as that point. From there on to Buffalo he paid and paid again, and he also paid for any meals and any lodging he had along the way. This slickering quickly made forwarding houses a public scandal. State laws soon made it difficult for them to operate brazenly, so they merely changed their spots and their tactics somewhat and prepared for the gigantic business of handling, in one way or another, a large part of the great immigration from Europe, principally from Ireland and Germany, that was getting into full flood by the end of the 1840's. But by then the more forward-looking of the railroads were establishing their own agencies for the encouragement of emigration from Europe to America and specifically to the gorgeous country along the lines of the railroads immediately interested in settlers.

The panic of 1837 was doubtless a good thing for a more orderly advance of railroads. It had taken a terrible toll. Poor's *Railroad Manual* noted that many roads, especially in the West and South, were abandoned, while others which had never from the day work began paid even the cost of construction were thrown into bankruptcy. It is probable that this was the proper end for these roads. Yet, railroad fever, after its almost deadly setback during the panic, returned to circulation with greater strength, and with better balance, than ever before.

Growing Pains

By turns the railroad was to bedevil and bewilder America. In one of his essays Herbert Spencer, an Englishman who meant more to the United States than to his native land and who thoroughly believed in Steam, said that a volume would be required simply to trace through all of its ramifications the effects contingent upon the act of lighting a fire. These effects, he vowed, were infinite though imperceptible. The effects upon the United States of steam, which comes from water heated over a fire, are also infinite, but most of them are easily perceptible.

For one thing, steam locomotion in the United States harmed one region to build up another. The forces of nature meant little to it. It overcame wind and tide. It abolished the Mississippi River, until then a gigantic fact. It abolished those fearful reaches of the interior that cartographers labeled Great American Desert. All that even the Rockies meant to steam locomotion was merely a little more fire under the boiler.

Steam turned out to be capricious. It proved to be as much a master of what Americans called their Destiny as it was its slave. It carried the individual wherever he would go; and it carried away whole communities who did not want to go anywhere at all. Either that, or it buried them where they were. The railroad made bright green grass to grow in the once busy streets of Nantucket, Salem, and Charleston. It stole, openly and arrogantly, from New Orleans that monopoly of wealth which the Mississippi once promised to pour into her lap. Up in the hills of Vermont and New Hampshire, pine and spruce started to creep across the fields and pastures of deserted farms, to surround even the barns and houses and to strangle them—all because of steam locomotion. . . .

Steam locomotion was filled with wayward fancies. For some mysterious reason that only professors of economics pretend to understand, it carried wealth and importance past one place to lay them down at another. It passed Oswego, Dunkirk, Sandusky, and Fort Wayne to build a gigantic city at the foot of Lake Michigan. It picked the most impossible building site in California and conjured up San Francisco on the spot. It whistled past old and important places like Fort Vancouver, Tumwater, and Nisqually and made secondary hamlets like Portland and Seattle into cities.

There was no telling what steam would do, and many a fortune was made or lost because of its perversity. Before men realized what was going on, steam had moved the center of population from near the Atlantic seaboard to a point that existed in the school books of the same generation only as deep wilderness. More than one pioneer related, in no more than his middle years, how the last Indian whoop and the last sad cadence of the owl had died in the echo of the first locomotive. Wilderness one year, metropolis the next. . . .

Minneapolis, Portland, and Seattle grew up so rapidly they left the map makers a full ten years, perhaps twenty years, in the rear; while all along the two thousand miles separating those places there grew up one, then two, then three lines of continuous civilization, bolstered on each side by rectangular townships devoted to growing wheat, mining copper, cutting timber—now that wheat, copper, and lumber could be taken to market. "All that land," said a congressman referring to the entire American West, "wasn't worth ten cents until the railroads came."

It was the same everywhere in the country. Following the Civil War the United States started to build so rapidly, so madly, and continued to the end of the century in such a frenzy of exploitation, that it might have wrecked itself had it not been for the railroad. The country did crack several times, but it never quite blew up, or collapsed, and the reason it not only survived but prospered in wealth, in population, and in power was the railroad. Charles Francis Adams, our great philosopher of railroads, said it. "The simple truth was," he wrote, "that through its energetic railroad development, the country was then producing real wealth as no country ever produced it before. Behind all the artificial inflation which . . . so clearly foreshadowed a catastrophe, there was also going on a production that exceeded all experience."

The new element of the railroad, Adams believed, did away with the best of reasoned conclusions. Acting upon undeveloped and almost inexhaustible natural resources, it dragged the country through its difficulties in spite of itself—as if all the fraud, the ignorance, and speculation that greedy men could think up and practice were quite unable, because of the railroad, to precipitate disaster. Every mile of steel laid was quietly adding many times its cost to the aggregate wealth of the country. . . .

Although Mr. Adams did not say so, the building of the American railroad system was one of the greatest dramas of modern times. Unlike the Republic itself, whose founding can be dated well enough for all practical and symbolic purposes as of July 4, 1776, the American railroad system cannot be said to have a birthday. For many years it existed only in the minds of a few visionaries who, try as they did, could make little impression on the great mass of Americans, just then charmed by the wonders of canals. The greatest of these visionaries, or prophets, was an odd genius named Oliver Evans who soon after the Revolution petitioned at least two legislatures for exclusive rights to use what he termed his "improvements in stream carriages" in their states.

A few other prophets were stirring, among them John Stevens of Hoboken, who built a miniature locomotive, which he ran around on a track in the yard of his home. The states of New Jersey and Pennsylvania good-naturedly granted Stevens the charters he wanted, which proposed to build a railroad across those states. Stevens was a veteran of the Revolution, hence they humored him, knowing nothing would come of his aberrations. And nothing did, though the noise he made did prompt a group of Pennsylvanians to send William Strickland to England to learn what he could about the new steam railways there.

England had taken to the steam engine, especially in its locomotive form, with a readiness that seems to have been lacking in America. News of the first English railroads came across the sea, and Strickland and other Americans had seen with their own eyes what was going on. Like an imported virus, the idea at last began to function in American port towns. In 1827 a group of citizens incorporated the Baltimore & Ohio Rail Road Company, and a bit later prevailed on old Charles Carroll, sole surviving Signer of the Declaration, to lean on a spade and turn a sod, while a band played and cannon boomed. In quick succession other railroad companies were organized in New York, Philadelphia, and Charleston.

Boston already had a railroad of a sort, three miles of wooden rails laid on stone ties to move granite from Quincy to the banks of the Neponset River, where the stones would be transported by water to Charlestown, there to form the Bunker Hill Monument. Horses were its motive power. Nor was the Baltimore & Ohio quite ready to take the big step to steam. They fooled around with sail cars and with horsepower in its direct and in its treadmill form. In Charleston, South Carolina, however, a group of railroad builders engaged Horatio Allen, who wanted steam, to run their line. Allen had the first American-built locomotive made in New York and hoisted it aboard his rails where, in December 1830, it pulled the first train of cars ever moved by steam in the United States. This six miles of railroad may properly be said to have fathered all lines since in this country. It was more the true source than the much-heralded, much-pictured race between Peter Cooper's *Tom Thumb* engine and a gray horse, the horse winning hands down.

The success of the South Carolina railroad brought a rash of incorporations in all of the settled regions except New England where, so solid Yankees said, commerce was tied to the sea and always would be. By 1840 there were almost five thousand miles of steam railroad in the United States, of which Pennsylvania had almost one fifth, with New York second on the list, followed by Virginia, North Carolina, Alabama, Tennessee, and Louisiana.

In the meantime, competing philosophers had emerged from their lairs to argue what a railroad was. Some said it was merely an improved turnpike, a semipublic way over which, by the payment of a fee, any man might operate his steam engine and carriages. If this contention seems odd today, it did not seem odd to a people who were familiar with turnpikes but had never seen a steam railroad. Other philosophers contended that a railroad was not and could not, with impunity, be considered a turnpike. Chief of this school was the remarkable Jonathan Knight, civil engineer who surveyed for the Chesapeake & Ohio Canal Company, laid out the Federal Government's National Road, then became engineer for the Baltimore & Ohio. A railroad, he said, could not operate successfully if more than one company ran steam carriages upon it. Since that day Knight's basic philosophy of single owner-ship has remained unchanged, although on thousands of miles of track more than one railroad operates trains on a rent or lease arrangement.

In the wake of the prophets came the incorporators of railroads. Incorporators were not necessarily builders. Many of these men were simply gull-catchers who had previously discovered easy money in selling stock in companies ostensibly formed for the purpose of digging canals, or building plank roads. The canals were never dug, the planks never laid, and now their railroads were never built. How numerous were these crooks is to be judged by the expression that became current if not popular: "As worthless as railroad stock."

But there were also honest and capable men among the organizers of railroad companies, men who at last had caught the vision of the steam locomotive, and they worked to some purpose to lay the first lines of iron rails. Conservatives were seldom among them. Conservatives at first paid the railroad no heed at all, but presently they roused and in the manner of their kind time out of mind, they fought the innovation. Enlisting both the law and the clergy, to say nothing of hired free-lance orators and makers of "Railroad Disaster" lithographs, the conservatives, or merely the owners of canal stock and stagecoach lines acting like conservatives, fought the railroad with every means ingenious men could devise.

They had lost, of course, before they started to fight. On went the rails, connecting two towns here, another two towns there, and over the rails went dinkey little engines hauling either stagecoaches with flanged wheels, or long boxes. Steam-railroad travel was a novelty, but it was hardly pleasure. No one ever knew, when a brigade of cars left a depot, when or if it would arrive at the other terminal. Farmers piled logs across the tracks. Bulls at pasture, offended by the sight of the puffing engines, charged them head on and butted them from the rails —until Isaac Dripps, boss mechanic of the Camden & Amboy, invented the deadly parent of all cowcatchers, which *speared* the rambunctious bulls and tamed them somewhat.

Passengers discovered they not only had to pay to ride on the cars; they had often to help lift them back onto the rails and to push entire trains over slight grades. Smoke sooted them, cinders burned their broadcloth and bombazine, yet there was no keeping them from riding behind what was soon heralded as the Iron Horse, the animal that was going to change and make America.

Men of outstanding imagination and ability were presently showing interest in the railroad. John Edgar Thomson took hold of the newly formed Pennsylvania Railroad, added a dilapidated line here and there, purchased a state-owned streak of rust, and set his own crews to laying track from Harrisburg to Pittsburgh. When he died in 1874, his road was one of the great systems in the country. Erastus Corning, nail maker of Albany, New York, and associates, got a pot of cash together, purchased ten small railroads, then forged them into the New York Central, one of the wonders of the time. Up in now waking New England, John Poor, on foot and in sleigh, set out to find a route from Portland to Montreal, and then with efforts to be described only as epic, built what became the Grand Trunk. In Georgia, in Tennessee, in Ohio, even in far Minnesota, men of push and determination were connecting their towns with other towns, or with rivers or lakes, laying rails, buying rolling stock, naming their roads ". . . & Pacific" with a superb indifference to the two thousand or more miles that stretched out beyond the farthest western railhead.

The challenge of the plains and mountains, however, was to be met. Brisk men in New York and California asked the government to help them bridge the continent, and the government donated land and a lot of money and sent soldiers to protect the construction crews from the dismayed Indians who knew well enough what the Iron Horse would do to their buffalo. The Union and the Central Pacific outfits went to work at both ends, making fortunes for a few, impoverishing many more, seducing senators and other noble statesmen into what one voluble critic said were "cunning, craft, chicane, guile, and knavery"; yet, in the end, providing the United States with a steel highway of incalculable value. When impassioned orators spoke of this first transcontinental as a Path of Empire, they were not speaking bombast; it was sober truth. . . .

In a little more than two decades, three transcontinental railroads were built with government help. All three wound up in bankruptcy courts. And thus, when James Jerome Hill said he was going to build a line from the Great Lakes to Puget Sound, without government cash or land grant, even his close friends thought him mad. But his Great Northern arrived at Puget Sound without a penny of Federal help, nor did it fail. It was an achievement to shame the much-touted construction of the Erie canal.

Along with the era of feverish construction went the era of buccaneering. Perhaps Uncle Dan'l Drew started it. Perhaps he merely gave it impetus. In any case this drover of cattle who salted his steers, then let them drink their fill before weighing—thus giving us Watered Stock—turned his great talents to railroad speculation, trying his hand first on the New York & Erie. "I got to be a millionaire afore I knowed it, hardly," he liked to say. And so he did. With Jay Gould and Jim Fisk, Jr., Drew wrecked the Erie again and again, and tried to wreck the New York & Harlem, running plumb into old Commodore Vanderbilt, who was too much for him. After looting here and there for more than a decade, Uncle Dan'l softened to the extent of setting aside suitable sums, in the style of so many rascals, for the founding of seminaries of God.

The old Commodore used methods akin to Drew's, yet on an even grander scale, and was so eminently successful that the vast New York Central system, which he and his son William H. built out of lines they clubbed into compliance, was often known simply as Mr. V's Road. Both father and son were of outstanding ability in the business of amalgamating and operating railroads, even though the younger man has been continuously discredited because of a statement which, honest though it was and quite reasonable from his point of view, proved most offensive to the public; for sixty years it has been used against Capital in all its forms. "The public be damned!" said the younger Mr. Vanderbilt. . . .

Raids similar to those of Drew, Gould, and Vanderbilt were being staged in the West. Out where the deer and the antelope are said to play, Ben Holladay, Henry Villard, and a number of other go-getting men were fighting for control of rails and boats in the Pacific Northwest; and the war proved so wide and bitter that reverberations were felt in England, Germany, and Austria, where Lords and Junkers began to wonder why the laying of simple American iron rails could cost so much good European money.

In California a quartet of singularly grasping men named Crocker, Huntington, Stanford, and Hopkins, commonly known as the Big Four, were using the courts, the legislatures, and hundreds of gunmen to build a monopoly out of the Southern Pacific, the Central Pacific, and sundry lines bought under pressure. Fighting the Big Four in the Southwest were the men of the Santa Fe, virtually a Yankee railroad, owned and run from Boston, operating in the most remote region possible. . . .

Let one not forget . . . that it was these ruthless railroad builders and operators, whose morals and principles were average but whose abilities were very great—that it was these men, perhaps more than any other class, who were making the United States into the first industrial nation on earth, ready to take her place in world councils on any subject, whether of commerce or war. If these industrialists are to be damned, and I say they *are* to be damned, it is not because of what they did, but what they didn't do. The world they were building had little place in it for the artist of painting, of letters, of music, nor for the thinker who was other than pragmatic. Let them be damned and doubledamned for these shortcomings, but not because they rode roughshod over their fellows.

With America building so frantically, it was natural that the cost came high. You do not get speed except at an extra cost. America paid for it in many ways, and is still paying.

It began to pay for speed, and greed, in the 1850 period, when disasters on the shoddy and hurrying railroads became a disgrace. With heavy irony *Harper's Weekly* of June 31, 1858, said it:

> Nobody's murders. The railroads are insatiable. Boilers are bursting all over the country—railroad bridges are breaking and rails snapping—human life is sadly and foolishly squandered—but nobody is to blame. Boilers burst themselves. Rails break themselves. And it may be questioned whether the consequent slaughter of men, women and children is not really suicide. . . .

Those were harsh words, from Mr. Harper's periodical, yet no harsher than conditions warranted, as the State of New York discovered when it made an investigation into the operating practices of its railroads. It learned that a difference of at least five minutes was to be expected of the watches of engineer and conductor. It found that a train might expect to encounter an unguarded and wide-open drawbridge either by day or by night, and that an engineer might well run his train on the supposition he would find another train out of its scheduled running order at any old place along the line. So careless had locomotive engineers become and so erratic their rolling stock, that No. 238 of the 250 regulations that an alarmed New York saw fit to set up, required that "The engineman must invariably start with care and see that he has his whole train before he gets beyond the limits of the station."

First Connecticut, then New York, then other states, desperate at the horrors committed almost daily by the railroads, attempted to stay the slaughter. Regulations tumbled out of the legislative committees like a snow storm—and had little more effect. True, equipment did improve simply from necessity; rails were made better and heavier for the same reason. Humanitarianism did not enter into it. But inventors were busy. [Eli Hamilton] Janney and his automatic coupler and other devices, [George] Westinghouse with his air brake, they and a thousand other gadgeteers were offering the roads marvelous or indifferent or hopeless ideas. Janney and Westinghouse made an impression, but their fine devices were used sparingly until the fanatic Alonzo Coffin arose to cry aloud at the murder, and to club the railroads and the government until the Interstate Commerce Commission came into being and forced the automatic coupler and air brake on the recalcitrant railroads. . . . The forming of the Interstate Commerce Commission, stemming from the Granger movement, . . . helped the carriers to improve their morals and also to protect their employees from needless injury. As for the employees, they were helping themselves, organizing first one Brotherhood, then another, staging or taking part in strikes only when they felt nothing else would do; but when they did strike, they struck with desperate determination. The years 1877 and 1894 were wreathed in the smoke of burning cars and gunpowder, while would-be travelers stayed at home and little freight moved. Out of the violence the railroad unions emerged both strong and stable, to be of immeasurable help in making railroad employees dependable, self-reliant, well-paid, and efficient. For a long period hard liquor was the greatest enemy to good railroad operation. Education and pressure, both by the unions and the carriers, plus the celebrated Rule G [which called for instant dismissal for use of intoxicants while on duty] brought such sobriety that for a long time past few Americans have seen a drunken railroad man on duty.

Railroads permeated every last corner of American geography and mind. The trunk lines stretched out to reach Chicago, to reach the Gulf, to reach the West Coast. Branch lines came to the main lines in patterns like the ribs to a fish's backbone. And before the great period of construction had reached its climax, stub lines forked off from branch lines until one would have been hard put to trace all the relationships. Into the second decade of the twentieth century new rails were being laid, although by then, too, many a branch line was finding the going difficult indeed; and soon they were fading, one after the other, as the internal combustion engine took hold of America and started to change its habits once more, just as the rails had changed things seventy-five years before.

A huge book, set in fine type, would not find room even to list the countless occupations brought into being by the railroads. All railroad jobs were, of course, new occupations, and so were many jobs merely associated with railroads. Express service was virtually unknown until a few men like William Harnden, Daniel Niles, and Alvin Adams took to riding the steam cars, carrying inside their tall beaver hats the important and valuable parcels of businessmen who did not like the slowness of the mails, nor consider the post office wholly reliable. The individual express men filled a real need. In a little while their business was such as to require them to carry carpetbags, then trunks, until finally they were renting whole cars and the express business became of great importance to the railroads.

The Federal Government did not favor express companies [see "Packages and Pullmans," in this section, below] and for a considerable period harassed them as lawbreakers; yet, because express did fill a need, it grew famously in spite of all objections and probably had an influence in forcing Uncle Sam to give better service with his mails. The Fast Mail came into being. All America was greatly excited and immensely pleased to see mailbags snatched from stanchions at little depots by the iron arm of the mail car while the train thundered by in full flight. Mail cars were painted prettily. They were marked with the symbol of the Union, flying with her own wings. The Fast Mail train itself was a grand symbol of Progress in an age that was certain Progress led, if not to Utopia, then to a fine condition of things anyway.

In these handsome cars rode young men who sorted letters and papers while the train rolled through the night, while it spanned rivers and crossed mountains, speeding the correspondence of the nation, bringing the far outposts on the Pacific shore twenty-four hours closer to the old settled regions. It was wonderful, and any man who doubted the future was no man to live in America. . . .

Other jobs, too, stemmed from the rails, among them jobs to be filled by hundreds of boys and young men who were known as train boys or news butchers, half salesmen, half carnival folk, who walked the rolling trains and hawked their wares, supplying the latest news to literates, and the Facts of Life to adolescents in the form of *Only a Boy* and the snappy *Paris Package,* not to be opened in the cars, and tons of salted peanuts and chewing gum to ruminants.

Telegraphy did not come into its own until its conjunction with the railroad. . . . Telegraphers soon were a race apart, a fraternity comparable to that of the tramp printers in some respects, yet leading to better things. More than one railroad president got his start pounding a key at some obscure junction or way station.

Inspired by the new railroads, the Reno brothers of Indiana invented the profession of train robber, highly thought of and much romanticized for a hundred years, due in part to the spectacular professional technique developed by members of the James and Younger families, together with the hard-riding Daltons. . . .

Hero though the train robber was to much of America, an even greater hero was the Brave Engineer, the man in the right-hand side of the locomotive cab, who drove his train safely through night and storm; or tragically into some other train, or washout, or defective bridge or rail. The Brave Engineer largely supplanted the Soldier and the Sailor as what Young America wanted to be when he grew up. Keen-eyed, tanned to leather by the elements that constantly played upon him, the lines in his face marked with soot, the engineer always looked ahead, scanning the bright rails for danger, his mind weighted with responsibility for his charges in the cars, his left arm resting on the throttle. It was his duty to put her through, or to die at his post, and die he too often did, to go into balladry along with the boy upon the burning deck and the kind if inefficient skipper of the doomed *Hesperus.*

He was a great, a magnificent figure to Young America. More than one banker and college president and eminent divine envied him, too, for his was the post they all had wanted and once meant to have, the calling for which superb whistles blew and noble bells rang, to the accompaniment of pounding drivers on the rails. He was the man who put her through, come what might of the weather or other deviltry.

Time was his very god, this man. No matter what the time-card showed, no matter how able the officials, the division super-intendents, the dispatchers, switchmen, and fireman, it was at last and finally the engineer who put her through on time. With the coming of the railroad, Time for the first time in history really became an important measure in the lives of most Americans. To be "on time" was "railroad fashion."

UP FROM THE WOOD BURNERS [3]

The earlier period of railway development was a period of pioneering, a period of rapid expansion, when lines were being pushed into virgin territory. Railway mileage increased rapidly during that period. When the country had been covered with a network of rail lines, expansion in new territory was virtually at an end. But with extensive agricultural and industrial growth of the territory served by the railroads, the need for intensive development of existing lines increased. Therefore, in the last third of a century the railroads have been engaged primarily in increasing the capacity and efficiency of the existing plant.

The railroads have not only increased their capacity through the construction of multiple tracks, additional yard tracks and sidings, industry tracks, larger shops, more powerful and more efficient locomotives, larger and better cars, improved signal and communication systems, the introduction of electronic devices, and so on, but they have improved their facilities in countless ways in the interest of increased comfort, convenience, speed, safety, and efficiency. . . .

The Association of American Railroads and its predecessor organizations, forming the central research and coordinating agencies of the railway industry, are credited with many of the improvements which have marked railway developments during the last three quarters of a century. [A history of the development of American railroads would be incomplete without reference to the part played by the Association of American Railroads and its predecessors in the unification, standardization,

[3] From *American Railroads, Their Growth and Development* (p 19-32) and *Quiz On Railroads and Railroading* (unpaged). Association of American Railroads. Transportation Building. Washington 6, D.C. '58. Used by permission.

and coordination of railway operations and practices. Shortly after the Civil War the railroads began to coordinate certain of their activities through meetings, conventions, and associations organized for the purpose of accomplishing certain things jointly which could not be done by individual roads working separately. The name of the Association of American Railroads is comparatively new but it is the lineal descendant of the Master Car Builders' Association, formed in 1867 to conduct experiments looking toward the standardization of freight cars; the General Time Convention of Railway Managers, which pioneered our system of Standard Time; and the Railway Association of America, formed in 1873 for the purpose of standardizing railway operations. These and other organizations of railroad men are now parts of the Association of American Railroads, which was created in 1934 by the merger of the American Railway Association, the Association of Railway Executives, and other organizations with similar interests.—Ed.]

One of the first of these improvements was the adoption of Standard Time. [See "Two Noons on Sunday" in this section, below.]. . . Another was the standardization of gauge of tracks and equipment. In 1871, there were no fewer than twenty-three different railway gauges in use to a greater or lesser extent in this country. The widest of these gauges was six feet; the narrowest was three feet. (Later, a few two-foot gauge roads were built.) Obviously, the standardization of gauge was a major undertaking, due to the fact that locomotives and cars, as well as track, had to be converted. But through joint effort and teamwork, standardization of gauge, with minor exceptions, became an accomplished fact in 1886.

Among the many other important results of joint action . . . was the adoption of a Standard Code of Operating Rules by railroads throughout the country, uniform codes governing the operation of block signals and interlocking devices, and the interchange and hire of freight cars, per diem, and demurrage.

Joint studies and research also contributed greatly to the development of locomotives and cars, the air brake, the automatic coupler, automatic signals, improved communications, including train radio, and the adoption of engineering standards applying to bridges, rails, ties, and other parts of the railway track structure. . . . [Today] any shipper anywhere in the United States, Canada, Mexico, and Cuba can load a freight car for delivery at any other railway station in these four countries. This fact, which is the basis of continent-wide commerce, is largely due to the joint efforts of the railroads. . . .

The Railroad Organization

Each railroad company shapes its organization to fit its particular requirements. A small railroad may have only a few officers and employees and a very simple departmental set-up. A large railroad company, with many thousands of employees and doing a business of many millions of dollars annually, has a much more extensive organization, with several major departments and many minor departments, divisions and bureaus.

Generally speaking, a railroad is organized departmentally as follows:

The Executive Department is headed by the President and includes his staff of assistants. The President is the responsible head of the railroad organization. He is accountable to the Board of Directors and to the stockholders for the property and its efficient operation.

The Operating Department, usually headed by a Vice President or General Manager is, with respect to the number of persons employed, the largest department of a railroad. This department operates the trains, the yards, the freight and passenger stations, and usually attends to the maintenance of the railroad plant.

Under the Operating Vice President on the larger railroads are the General Manager, General Superintendents in charge of regions, the Superintendents in charge of divisions, and officers having charge of transportation, motive power, communications, signals, construction and maintenance.

Operating Department functions may be divided into three principal branches or departments: (1) transportation, (2) mechanical, and (3) engineering and maintenance. These are described briefly as follows:

Transportation. This branch of the Operating Department, usually under a Superintendent or a General Superintendent of Transportation, is responsible for the operation of trains, yards and stations. For operation purposes, the railroad is divided into divisions, each under a Superintendent. He is assisted by trainmasters, who have direct charge of train operations; yard-masters, who have charge of train and car movements in yards and terminals; and stationmasters and agents in charge of freight and passenger stations.

Mechanical. The staff is usually headed by a Chief Mechanical Officer, a Superintendent of Motive Power, or, on smaller roads, a Master Mechanic, under whom are foremen in charge of engine houses, car and locomotive shops, and inspectors of motive power and cars. The functions of this branch of the department are primarily the construction, repair, inspection and servicing of locomotives, cars, floating equipment, and work equipment, and the operation of shops, roundhouses, and other mechanical facilities for performing such activities.

Engineering. The staff is usually headed by a Chief Engineer. The functions of this branch of the department include the construction, reconstruction and maintenance of tracks, bridges, trestles, tunnels, shops, storehouses, signals, fences, stations, and other fixed properties. Responsibility for the upkeep, renewal and inspection of fixed property rests with the engineer maintenance of way, the engineer of buildings, and the engineer of bridges—all reporting to the Chief Engineer. For maintenance purposes, the roadway is divided into divisions, districts, and sections, with division engineers or roadmasters in charge of divisions, road supervisors in charge of districts, and section foremen in charge of sections. On some railroads the Engineering Department is independent of the Operating Department, its head reporting directly to the President of the railroad.

The Traffic Department, usually headed by a Vice President or Chief Traffic Officer, is the "sales department" of the railroad, having charge of the procurement of freight and passenger business. The department is usually divided into two sections, one dealing with freight matters and the other dealing with passenger matters.

Other important functions of the Traffic Department are the formulation of proposals for freight rates and passenger fares, the publication and distribution of tariffs or rate schedules, the presentation of testimony on rates before rate regulating bodies, the classification of freight through joint bureaus and committees, the planning, in conjunction with operating officers, of freight and passenger train schedules, and the preparation and publication of timetables and advertising material. The promotion of agricultural and industrial development in the railroad's territory is still another important function of the Traffic Department.

The Law Department, usually headed by a Vice President or a General Counsel, is responsible for the proper handling of all matters in which special knowledge of law is required. It not only handles matters before courts, state railroad commissions, the Interstate Commerce Commission and legislative committees, but also all other law matters such as the drafting of contracts and agreements, deeds and other documents. The head of the Law Department usually has, in addition to his regular duties, general supervision over tax matters and the settlement of personal injury and property damage claims.

The Accounting Department, usually headed by a Vice President, Comptroller, or a General Auditor, performs the vast accounting work required in connection with railroad operations. It portrays in figures the operations of the railroad and its financial position. The auditing of departmental and station accounts, bills, vouchers and payrolls, the compilation of statistics, and the preparation of statistical and financial reports are among the numerous duties of this department.

The Treasury Department, headed by the Treasurer of the company, receives and disburses money, checks and vouchers, issues or approves checks and vouchers, attends to the banking, issues pay-checks, pays dividends on the company's stock and interest on its bonds, and performs numerous other duties having to do with the financial affairs of the railroad.

The Purchasing and Stores Department does the buying and handles the storage and distribution of materials and supplies for the railroad. This department is usually headed by a Vice President or a Purchasing Agent. Serving under him are assistant purchasing agents or buyers, a general storekeeper, and division storekeepers. This department is charged with the responsibility of keeping the railroad supplied with thousands upon thousands of different materials and articles. It attends to the proper storage and distribution of materials, keeps the inventories, places orders, fills requisitions, issues vouchers and performs numerous other duties incident to buying, storing and distributing fuel, materials and supplies required for the efficient operation of the railroad.

Progress on Rails

No feature of railroading has been subjected to greater study on the part of engineers and metallurgists than the rails over which the heavy trains roll. To most people, the rail of today might appear to be the same as that of years ago. But it is heavier, stronger, more durable, and much safer.

The first railroads in this country were constructed of wooden rails upon which were fastened thin strips of iron to provide a running surface for the wheels. Iron rails, many of which were imported from England, gradually replaced wooden rails. The weight of these iron rails was about 50 to 56 pounds to the yard.

The first steel rail was rolled in this country in 1865, and in the 1870's steel came into extensive use. By the late 1890's it had almost entirely replaced iron. As weights of locomotives and cars increased and methods of rail manufacture were improved, the weight of rails increased. Today's steel rails—much superior to those of even a short generation ago—range in weight from

85 to 155 pounds per yard. The average weight of main line railroad rail is now almost 105 pounds per yard.

The length of rail has also been increased from time to time. The earliest strap-rail was 8 or 10 feet in length. By 1850, rail 18 and 20 feet in length was common. In 1920, the standard length was 33 feet. The present standard length is 39 feet, but some railroads use rails 60 to 78 feet long in special locations. In fact, some railroads are now using "continuous" rail—rail that has its joints welded together into lengths of a mile or more. The longest continuous welded rail in use in the United States in 1958 was 33,792 feet. There are many stretches of continuous rail exceeding a mile in length.

Evolution of Locomotives

Probably no part of the railway plant better illustrates the evolution of railroads and railroading than the locomotive. The earliest locomotives in this country weighed only a few tons each. Some of these little engines had upright boilers; others had horizontal boilers and horizontal cylinders.

Engines soon passed from the experimental to the practical stage, and the high-stacked wood-burners of the 1850's, although comparatively insignificant in size, began to resemble somewhat the steam locomotives with which most Americans are familiar. As standardization went forward, locomotives increased greatly in size and power.

The electric locomotive made its appearance in 1895, and by 1945 more than 6,000 miles of track had been electrified. An electric locomotive obtains its power from overhead lines, or from a "third rail" supplied with electricity from a distant generating station. The overhead structure on an electrified railroad, known as a catenary system, holds the electrically charged contact wire in firm level position above the track. Electric current from the overhead contact wire is transmitted to the locomotive through a retractable collecting device called a pantograph.

With the third-rail system, the electric current for the locomotive or motor car unit is transmitted through a metal contact shoe which slides along the charged third rail, just outside the running rails. Battery locomotives are used to a limited extent.

One of the most significant developments in the railroad field in recent years has been the trend toward dieselization of motive power. The Diesel engine was the invention of Dr. Rudolf Diesel, a mechanical engineer, who was born in France of German parentage in 1858 and disappeared mysteriously while crossing the English Channel en route to London in 1913. Dr. Diesel built his first model in 1892, and narrowly escaped death in trying to start it. His first successful Diesel engine (a single-cylinder, 25 horsepower unit), completed in 1897, attracted world-wide attention. The American rights to manufacture were purchased by Adolphus Busch of St. Louis in 1898, and the first Diesel engine built in this country was completed in September of that year.

A Diesel locomotive unit is a mobile power plant resting on a single frame, capable either of independent propulsion or of propulsion through a connected unit. Locomotive units are of two general types—designated as "A" and "B" units. An "A" unit is equipped for use singly or as a lead unit in a locomotive combination. A "B" unit is capable of only limited independent propulsion and is not equipped with the necessary appurtenances for use singly or as a lead unit in a locomotive combination. A Diesel locomotive may consist of one "A" locomotive unit operated singly or it may consist of two, three or four "A" and "B" locomotive units coupled and operated in combination to provide motive power for a train. [Since this motive power is applied to the driving wheels through an electric generator powered by the Diesel engine and not directly from it, railway units are generally referred to as Diesel-electric locomotives rather than simply Diesel locomotives.]

The power of Diesel-electric locomotive units ranges all the way from 400 to 2,400 horsepower, the great majority of those in freight and passenger service being 1,500 to 2,000 horsepower. Two 1,500-horsepower locomotive units coupled together produce a locomotive of 3,000 horsepower; three such units coupled together provide a locomotive of 4,500 horsepower; and four such units coupled together provide a locomotive of 6,000 horsepower. Steam for train heating is furnished by an oil-fired high-capacity steam generator. Generators of this type will evaporate up to 3,000 pounds of water per hour.

The first Diesel-electric locomotive was placed in switching service on an American railroad in October 1925, but it was not until 1934 that Diesel-electric locomotives were first used in passenger-train service. By 1941 they were being used in long-distance freight service. The most recent use of Diesel-electrics has been in commuter passenger-train service. At the end of World War II the railroads had in service 2,800 Diesel-electric locomotives, consisting of 3,645 units. At the end of 1957 these railroads were operating 27,186 Diesel-electric locomotive units.

New types of locomotives now in use include the gas-turbine electric locomotive and the ignitron rectifier electric freight locomotive.

The gas-turbine electric locomotive—packing a large amount of power in a comparatively small space—resembles a Diesel-electric locomotive in outward appearance. It burns low-grade, low-cost Bunker "C" fuel oil. It has an 8-axle B-B-B-B [8 driving axles] wheel arrangement with fully loaded weight of 66,500 pounds per axle. Started by an auxiliary Diesel engine, the gas-turbine is fired initially on Diesel oil and as idling speed is attained, Bunker "C" oil is introduced and the Diesel power is cut off, at which stage the starting mechanism automatically cuts off. Air is compressed to six times normal pressure by a shaft-driven axial-flow compressor. A turbine shaft drives the compressor and delivers 4,500 horsepower through a reduction gear to four DC generators, which in turn supply power to the eight traction motors. The locomotive is designed for fast, long-haul freight service.

The ignitron rectifier freight locomotive is an electric locomotive embodying a completely new principle. Single-phase AC power from the overhead trolley is rectified by means of sealed ignitron tubes, and the DC output of the rectifier is supplied to series-wound DC traction motors that drive the locomotive. Thus there is combined in one power unit the economies possible with an AC system of power distribution and the tractive advantages of DC motors. Except for the rectifier and associated circuits, the apparatus on the ignitron locomotive is similar to that on other electric locomotives. The locomotive develops 6,000 horsepower in two units. Each unit is rated at 3,000 rail horsepower and is driven through six 500-horsepower DC traction motors.

Atomic scientists and railway engineers are studying the possibilities of atomic power in the propulsion of locomotives. They freely predict that such a development is possible once the problem of shielding human life from radiation is solved. Whether atomic power would be more economical and efficient than present types of motive power is a question to which only further research can provide the answer.

Passenger Car Improvements

The first passenger cars were little more than stagecoaches mounted on flanged wheels. These were soon replaced by vehicles that looked like box cars with windows. Cars were lighted first by candles, then by oil lamps, and were heated by stoves. The earliest notable improvement in car building was the invention of an axle moving with the wheel instead of the wheel revolving on the axle. The wheels were then combined into a four-wheeled truck.

Gradually, passenger cars increased in size and comfort. Experiments with sleeping cars began as early as 1836. Stateroom cars were introduced in 1856. The first Pullman sleeping cars were placed in service in 1859 and 1865. The first dining cars were introduced in 1863, and in 1867 "hotel cars," combining sleeping and dining facilities, were placed in service. [See "Packages and Pullmans," in this section, below.]

By 1887, passengers were enjoying the comforts of steam heat and electric lights and had the security of the air brake, which replaced the hand brake. The old link-and-pin coupler was giving way to the safe and efficient automatic coupler. The built-in vestibule was invented in 1887, and the first train completely equipped with vestibules was placed in service that year. In 1903, steel-frame passenger cars were introduced, and in 1906 the first all-steel passenger coaches were placed in service, adding to the safety of train travel.

Passenger car developments in the present century include safety glass, fluorescent lighting, air conditioning, and streamlining. Reclining coach seats, roomette cars, café cars, lounge-parlor cars, tavern cars, coach sleepers, and glassed-in dome observation cars are features of the modern passenger train.

One of the outstanding developments of the 1930's was the introduction of streamlined passenger trains. The first successful streamliners were introduced in 1934. Such trains, constructed of alloys which are lighter and stronger than ordinary steel, are powered by Diesel-electric, electric and steam locomotives. The trains are designed and built to reduce air pressure or wind resistance as much as possible, and this, together with lightweight passenger cars, permits greater speed with a given amount of power.

Streamlined trains are air-conditioned to shut out dust, smoke, cinders, drafts, cold or heat, and provide clean, washed air at temperatures that assure passengers the maximum of comfort. With dust and smoke no longer a problem, the interior decorations and furnishings are done in cheerful and attractive color schemes. All-electric dining cars and dome dining cars are recent innovations.

Progress in Freight Service

Marked progress has also been made in freight equipment and in freight train operations. The earliest freight cars were of only a few tons' capacity. Modern freight cars are capable of carrying from 40 to 80 tons each. Some specially constructed cars are capable of carrying as much as 250 tons each. Modern freight cars are equipped with improved air brakes and automatic couplers. Wooden freight cars have been replaced by all-steel cars or by cars having steel underframes and steel framework. Among the latest innovations are freight cars constructed of stainless steel, aluminum, or light-weight alloys; compartment cars; aluminum container cars for small-lot shipments, cars equipped to carry highway trailers [see "Piggyback Riding," in Section III, below] and cars equipped with automatically regulated refrigerator systems.

The earliest known use of refrigeration by the railroads was in July 1851, when several tons of butter were shipped from Ogdensburg, New York, to Boston, Massachusetts, over what are now the Rutland and the Boston & Maine railroads. The shipment was in a wooden box car insulated with sawdust and stocked with ice. In 1857, fresh meats were shipped eastward from Chicago over the Michigan Central Railroad in box cars fitted with ice compartments at either end. With the increased manufacture of artificial ice, refrigeration became practical throughout the United States, greatly stimulating the production of fruits and vegetables, especially in the southern states. In the 1880's products grown in western and southern states were being marketed throughout the country.

The phenomenal growth of the market for frozen foods, which require intensive refrigeration in transit, has brought improved refrigerator cars built to standardized dimensions with provisions for easier riding at express train speeds. One of the latest developments is the mechanical refrigerator car, equipped with a self-contained, temperature-control refrigerator system, which provides zero temperatures when needed without servicing en route.

Refrigerated containers, weighing about 300 pounds when empty and holding about 500 pounds of commodities, are extensively used by the Railway Express Agency and several railway companies for less-than-carload shipments of seafoods, fresh meats, fruits, butter, and other perishables. Some railroads have large refrigerated containers designed to fit on special-type flat cars, three to the car. They are used in handling fresh meats and other perishables.

Where only two kinds of cars were once used—flat and box —modern freight equipment includes tank cars, refrigerator cars, open-top and closed-top gondola cars and hopper cars, container cars, automobile cars, furniture cars, ore cars, pulpwood cars, stock cars, poultry cars, and many other cars especially adapted for the transportation of every type of shipment.

PACKAGES AND PULLMANS [4]

The Railway Express

The sixteen-foot monument to William Frederick Harnden in Mount Auburn cemetery, Cambridge, Massachusetts, is probably deserved. Its legend states that Harnden was "Founder of the Express Business in America." Harnden died in 1845. The shaft was erected in 1856 by the combined effort of the express companies then in operation in the United States. If they credited Harnden as the Founder, then founder he was.

William Harnden was a native of Reading, Massachusetts. Weighing exactly one hundred pounds, and generally in poor health, he was one of those true monomaniacs who stick to an idea no matter the odds against them. When railroads at last got under way out of Boston, Harnden took a job as conductor on the Boston & Worcester. His working hours commonly ran to sixteen per day, and after three years, during which his health steadily became worse, he resigned. While looking around for something to do he made a trip to New York, where James Hale of Boston was building up a good business as a sort of informal express company for the Providence steamboat line. Bankers and merchants of Manhattan found Hale's service of use in sending packages of banknotes, bonds, and such to Boston.

Hale advised Harnden to set up as an express messenger between the two cities, carrying the packages himself. Ought to be a place for such a service, he said. Harnden consulted the steamboat company which granted him special rates between New York and Providence and even gave him what amounted to being an exclusive franchise. On the railroad between Providence and Worcester, however, the brothers Earle, B. D. and L. B., had been operating Earle's Express ever since the road opened in 1834, and Harnden could not obtain anything in the nature of an exclusive right. His relations with the Earles

[4] From *The Story of American Railroads,* by Stewart H. Holbrook, newspaperman and author of books on American historical subjects. This selection (from p 301-39 and p 317-26) is reprinted by permission of the publishers, Crown Publishers, New York. '47. Copyright 1947 by Crown Publishers.

must have been harmonious, for the two concerns used the same trains, and a bit later, after Harnden got under way, the Earles rented office space from him in Providence.

In February of 1839 Harnden was ready, and being a consistent believer in the power of newspapers, he inserted paid notices in the Boston and New York newspapers at once. In these advertisements Harnden used the word "express" in the meaning we use it today. He also made it a point to carry news dispatches or copies of newspapers for editors, doing this without charge and thus creating much goodwill in the inky sanctums. By late March the Boston *Transcript* was showing its appreciation by an editorial which spoke of Harnden's "honesty and fidelity" and went on to recommend "with much pleasure" his Express Service.

Although his friend Hale, in New York, worked hard to get all the business he could for Harnden, the amount at first was rather small. For several months a valise served to carry everything entrusted to the Harnden Express Company. Harnden was, in fact, about to give it up when the Cunard Line of Atlantic steamers went into operation between Boston and Liverpool. Business picked up immediately, chiefly through packages for New York and Philadelphia, which Harnden, with his brother Adolphus (now a member of the firm), could deliver much more quickly than if the stuff were left for transfer to the Boston & Providence road and the New York boat from Providence by the usual routine.

Harnden now added a messenger, Luke Damon, to make the run from Boston to New York and return by way of Stonington, Connecticut, and sent Dexter Brigham, a new partner, to England to establish a transatlantic express line and foreign-exchange business. Harnden went after business on the New York and Albany boats, and here he ran into the fact that the captains and pursers on the boats were making a good deal of money, on the side, by carrying letters and packages. Harnden could find no way to overcome this opposition until he made the acquaintance of Henry Wells, who appears to have had some influence with Daniel Drew, the sharp and cold-blooded riverboat magnate of the day. Wells, a Vermont Yankee, got Harnden an exclusive franchise for express on the New York-Albany boats; and Harnden appointed Wells his agent in Albany.

The Harnden Express Company now had a profitable triangle trade, between New York, Albany and Boston. Wells turned out to be an aggressive and competent agent. He urged Harnden to expand his service to the westward, to Buffalo, Cincinnati, even beyond, but the man wasn't interested. He apparently took little heed of the steady movement west of both old-stock Americans and new immigrants. Besides, competition was raising its head in many places, chiefly around Boston.

Typical of the new express lines following in the wake of the founder was Daniel Niles, for twenty years a stagecoach driver, who in January of 1842 took space in the Boston papers to announce that he had "commenced running an Express in connection with the Boston & Portland Railroad," and that he "solicits a share of the public patronage." . . .

Then, there was another outfit, Burke & Company's Express, which made its first messenger trip about a year after Harnden began. One of the partners was P. B. Burke, of whom history knows nothing, and the other was Alvin Adams, soon, though neither he nor Harnden knew it, to be one of the giants of the express business. . . . Alvin Adams was alert and determined. He was also a genial sort, and he like Harnden knew the value of the friendship of the press. He took pains to bring the latest New York papers to Boston editors, without charge and as quickly as possible, and he never thought of charging an editor for carrying a dispatch or even a personal letter. Adams also was expanding his business, first to New York by way of steamers from Stonington, then to Philadelphia. . . .

Meanwhile, and though he never showed any interest in invading the West, Harnden was doing a good deal to encourage immigration to the United States. Perhaps it was he who invented the system whereby new Irish and German immigrants in this country could pay the fare of kinsmen to Harnden's company, which would then attend to all details of bringing them over from Europe. Harnden was honest, too, in contrast to many of the so-called forwarding companies, and in time his offices were usually filled with brand-new immigrants waiting transportation to western states. Harnden got out posters and cards advertising this feature of his business, and appears to have been one of the few American agencies which did not set about to trim the new arrivals.

Then, in 1845, Harnden, worn out by illness, died, and the business was carried on by others until Adams & Company bought and converted it, with a number of other small concerns, into the Adams Express Company, destined for a long life.

Before Harnden died, his able Albany agent, Henry Wells, had gone into partnership with George E. Pomeroy to start an express service between Albany and Buffalo. . . . Among many other innovations they carried the first fresh oysters from New York to Buffalo and thus created a sensation, said Wells in later years, beyond description. Pomeroy & Company also contributed much to the reduction of charges of the United States Post Office for carrying letters, a feat of the first importance. The Post Office had been uneasy about the new express companies for some time. . . . Postmasters in all parts of the eastern states were beginning to grumble that the express men were taking away their life's blood. In 1841 the Post Office set investigators at work. They soon found that it was indeed true: the express concerns were carrying letters by the piece, by the package, and in great bundles. . . . The Postmaster General was worried not only because of the increasing number of express companies; he discovered without too much effort that businessmen and the public generally were in sympathy with the express men. It isn't difficult to understand why. In 1840 the United States charged from 6 to 25 cents for carrying a one-sheet letter, depending on distance, and the service was so slow and uncertain as to be the butt of comedians in print and variety hall. The Harnden and Adams companies would take a letter from New York to Boston for 12½ cents, half the rate of the Post Office. Pomeroy & Company had been doing a big business in letters, and early in 1843 this concern announced it would carry a letter anywhere in the country at a flat rate of

6 cents. Or, if you bought Pomeroy & Company stamps at 20 for $1, the rate was 5 cents.

It was time, said the Post Office Department, to put a stop to this "violation of law." It began to arrest Pomeroy & Company's messengers on the route between Albany and Buffalo, taking them off the trains and putting them into jail. Juries promptly acquitted them, despite their patent guilt. Pomeroy, to obviate the delays due to arrest of their young men, mounted them on fast horses and thus established the first Pony Express, its riders galloping across much of New York State, occasionally pursued by mounted government agents. The messengers were usually warned by citizens when the hated agents were nigh, and were guided across country to evade them. The businessmen of Rochester, to show how they stood in the matter, publicly offered outright aid of $6,000 a year to Pomeroy & Company if their agents would make daily trips to New York City. Proponents of the express companies argued that it was wrong for the government to seek to monopolize the carriage of mail. The Post Office countered by considering the taking over of all the express companies in business.

The government had to bow to public sentiment. In 1845 a bill was passed lowering postage rates to 5 cents for 300 miles, 10 cents to anywhere in the Union except the Pacific Coast states. At the same time the one-sheet rule was dropped. A letter was now an envelope and contents weighing not over one ounce. Pomeroy & Company presently retired from mail-carrying and became Livingston, Wells & Company. . . . The agent for Livingston, Wells at Buffalo was William G. Fargo, a native of Onondaga County, New York, who had previously worked for the Auburn & Syracuse railroad. Fargo was a young man of considerable vision, just the man to team with Wells, and on April 1, 1845, sure enough, Wells, Fargo and Dan Dunning organized the Western Express to handle business west of Buffalo. A year later Wells sold his interest in this firm to William A. Livingston, which became Livingston & Fargo, and went to live in Manhattan, there to manage Wells & Company.

The many small railroads between the Hudson and Lake Erie were rapidly being forged into the New York Central, and almost immediately an express company organized by John Butterfield, ex-stage driver, began to operate over the Central. Wells & Company had been paying Mr. Vanderbilt $100 a day for the privilege of having its express trunks and messenger ride from New York to Albany, and the new firm had to pay the same. This was obviously good for the Central and ruinous for the express companies. Being astute men, the Messrs. Wells, Livingston, Fargo, and Butterfield merged their outfits into two companies which, in turn, were made owners of another new concern, the American Express Company. This merger occurred in 1850.

Adams & Company had also been growing. . . . South went the Adams' tentacles, and West went those of the American. Chiefly through the alertness and imagination of the several Fargo brothers, all engaged with the American Express, that firm captured the Midwest while Adams was working south. The American service followed the Michigan Central as it crept into Chicago. It went on to occupy the Illinois Central, and the Chicago, Burlington & Quincy. Charles Fargo organized a line of Great Lakes steamers which the American soon took over. Presently an American agent had an office in Milwaukee, another in St. Paul.

Competition resulted in better services. . . . Express offices were enlarged and decorated in what the word of the era said was elegant taste. Uniforms appeared on certain employees. The trunks of messengers were prettied up. The collect-on-delivery shipment was invented. So was the use of waybills, in order to keep track of a package from the time of its acceptance to that of delivery.

Competition also had set off an epic fight to get and keep the fabulous business incident to the great gold strike in California. Adams got there first. Late in '49 Alvin Adams organized a new concern, Adams & Company of California, and put one of his partners, D. H. Haskell, late of Boston, in charge. Haskell opened offices in San Francisco on December 1st, and started express lines to Sacramento, and to Stockton, thus to cover both the northern and the southern diggings. For the next two and a half years Adams & Company worked up a tremendous business between the States and California, using the Panama, the Nicaragua and Cape Horn routes, steadily expanding its routes in California and into the Oregon country. It had competition, of course, but Adams managed to do more business than all of the small concerns put together.

In the middle of 1852 the up-and-coming American Express organized a subsidiary to act as its western ally, calling it Wells, Fargo & Company. The first thing Wells Fargo did was to open an ocean express service between New York and San Francisco, via Panama, and set the rate at 40 cents a pound, or 20 cents under the monopoly rate charged by Adams. It also built a gaudy office building in San Francisco, and began at once to buy out the small concerns whose routes it wanted. Both concerns now concentrated on speed. . . . Races between the two firms to get the latest eastern newspapers from the San Francisco docks to interior towns kept up the rivalry for business, and were followed with great interest by miners and others. Both outfits went into the letter-carrying trade, and Adams got out special 25-cent postage stamps. The Post Office Department cracked down in 1853 with an order that all letters carried by express must also carry United States postage. The order was obeyed to a certain extent, but the express companies, and particularly Wells Fargo, continued for many years to be the main reliance of pioneers for mail service in the remoter parts of the region.

Both concerns made a business of buying gold dust. Both operated banks. Adams & Company appear to have been rather careless in many things, including the losing of considerable quantities of gold dust. There were other banking firms, too, and in 1855 one of them, Page, Bacon & Company, underwent a run, started it was said because one of its drafts in the East had been dishonored. After paying out some $600,000, Page Bacon closed their doors. Public confidence, which had been undergoing pressure because of a number of small bank failures, was getting lower by the day, and runs now started on Adams, on Wells Fargo and other big banks. All closed their doors, and the city of San Francisco went into a panic. Almost two hundred business houses, with liabilities of $8 million, were forced to suspend. Adams and many another concern went into bankruptcy. Wells, Fargo & Company continued to pay all of their obligations. When the smoked had cleared from the panic, they were the dominant express company on the Pacific Coast, and so they remained until they lost their identity in merger with the American Express many years later.

The original Adams & Company was still in business in the East and South. Just before the shot was fired at Sumter in 1861, a new concern the Southern Express Company, suddenly took over all of the Adams business in seven southern states in what Alvin F. Harlow calls "one of the deepest and foggiest of all the mysteries" in the history of American express companies. The Southern served the Confederate Army faithfully throughout the war, while in the North, Adams & Company all but had a monopoly of serving the Army and other government agencies. For the next four years messengers for both companies often traveled in cars piled high with coffins that were occupied. As the Northern armies gradually overran the South, the Adams company took over the routes given up by the Southern; and in 1866 it turned back these routes to the Southern. . . .

For the most part the moguls of the express business became wealthy in a very short time, but nearly all of them continued to live without undue ostentation. It was said that by the 1870's express had made a hundred millionaires. Only one of them appears to have gone in for show. He was John Hoey who started as a clerk with Adams and rose to become general manager. Hoey built an atrocious mansion on Long Island, along with 130 acres of landscaped grounds, and went in for as vulgar a display of new wealth as the times could boast, thus causing many ordinarily unthinking people to believe there must be some money in the express business. Hoey the showoff, indeed, may have been an influence in the steadily mounting cry for regulation of the express companies.

Regulation was coming, too. As early as the 1880's a demand arose for a parcel post, operated by the government, to break the monopoly of the four great express concerns. The agitation never ceased for thirty years. The new Interstate Commerce Commission looked closely into the affairs of the express companies, then charged that they were guilty of double collections, exorbitant rates, unreasonable delays through indirect routings, excessive rates of insurance, and discrimination between shippers. Newspapers and magazines took up the cry. Cartoonists made the Express Trust of their pictures a fat, drooling ogre fit for the company of the fat drooling ogres of Steel, Meat, Sugar, and Railroads. In Congress, Senators Platt and Depew fought nobly against any regulation at all, but the pressure was becoming too great, and in 1913 government parcel post went into effect. At the same time Congress ordered express rates lowered. The stock values of all express companies declined.

The great and gouging days were over. . . . When America entered the war of 1917, the government took over the railroads and began to seize and use express cars for hauling troop baggage and other materials of war. A year later the government merged the existing express concerns into one company, which presently became known as the American Railway Express Company. Into it went the Adams, American, Southern, and Wells Fargo. . . .

The merged company ceased to exist in 1929 when it was bought by 86 railroads, which reorganized it into the form in which it is known today, the Railway Express Agency.

[The Agency is now owned by 69 railroad companies. Stock ownership, however, gives only voting privileges; it does not affect the distribution of revenue. In practice the Agency, as the agent of the railroads, files necessary tariffs, collects express charges from the public, deducts from these gross receipts all its own operating expenses, and distributes the balance among the various express-carrying railroads in proportion to the business handled by each of the 242 railroads operating under a standard contract.

The Agency is now a nation-wide system for the handling of express packages and less-than-carlot and carlot shipments requiring special handling. It conducts business through 14,000 offices serving 23,000 communities and uses in its operations more than 177,000 miles of railroad lines, 11,000 miles of boat lines, 143,000 miles of air lines, and 93,000 miles of motor-carrier lines. It employs over 42,000 persons and owns and operates a fleet of some 13,000 motor trucks for the pick-up and delivery of over 500,000 pieces of express each day. Through overseas agents it provides a world-wide, single-carrier express service.—Ed.]

The Story of the Sleeping Car

Years before there was any railroad in the country extensive enough to call for travel at night, inventive minds were at work on the notion of a sleeping car. In 1829 there appeared in Boston one R. F. Morgan of Stockbridge, Massachusetts, a man of many ideas regarding railroads. Three years previously he had surveyed, partly on his own and partly aided by funds from friends, a route for a railroad to run from Albany, New York, to Springfield, Massachusetts. As a surveyor he was pretty good, for his route turned out years later to be almost precisely that adopted by the Boston & Albany line.

Morgan also turned his attention to wheels for railroad cars, and presently designed such a free wheeling job that he claimed friction was reduced almost to nothing. It was this wheel idea that took him to Boston in 1829. There in Fanueil Hall he exhibited the wheel under auspices of the new and locally organized Rail Road Association. He also exhibited what was probably the first special design for a sleeping car. 'Twas a fearful thing to behold, this Morgan's Rail Road Carriage, a doubledecker so big that the reporter of the *American Traveller* of Boston termed it a land barge.

The upper level was to be a sort of promenade deck, complete with benches and covered with awning, and also containing what Morgan said was a "captain's office." The lower level was inclosed and contained five "births," a spelling the *Traveller* did not take the trouble to correct. And because in those days décor was an absolute necessity, a cupola rose beautifully from the stern of the top deck and was surmounted by an American flag. Apparently Morgan did not patent his land barge, but soon dropped it and went on to other things.

The idea of a sleeping car, with experiments in 1836-1837 on the Cumberland Valley R.R., continued to bemuse the minds of the countless Americans who were thinking up things for the new railroads, and in 1838 a plan for a sleeping car was actually patented by one Charles McGraw. Nothing seems to have come from Mr. McGraw's patent, although in the same year the Baltimore *Chronicle* reported that "cars intended for night travel" between that city and Philadelphia had gone into use. They were truly wonderful, said the *Chronicle,* for you could "go to rest in a pleasant berth, sleep as soundly as in your own bed at home, and on awakening next morning find yourself at the end of your journey, and in time to take your passage to New York if you are bent there." One need not be a cynic to doubt the basic accuracy of that statement.

It is doubtful, judging from a contemporary account, that sleeping cars had improved very much by 1843, when the New York & Erie railroad had two built and put into use. They were named the *Erie* and the *Ontario,* but they were known as the "diamond cars" because their windows were in that shape. The frames of the seats were stationary, the cushions loose. Two iron rods could be slid from under one seat and fitted into holes in the frame of the other seat, then the seat cushions moved onto the bars, and the back cushions moved down flat, the whole making a sort of couch. Incidentally, the cushions were of horsehair cloth, to which only the thickest clothing was impervious. There were no pillows or bedclothes, and travelers went to bed boots, saddles and all. But the Erie's diamond cars were found too heavy for use, and soon became boarding houses for track crews. (Though they were not successful, the Erie's diamond cars of 1843 played a part thirty-six years later.

When the Pullman company brought suit in 1879 for infringement against the Wagner Sleeping Car Company, it was "so nonplussed at revelations made in regard to the Erie sleeping cars of 1843, that a halt was called in the proceedings and both Pullman and Wagner concluded it would not do to stand a legal test of their rights, so they compromised and agreed to share in the profits of an invention which was old long before either of the claimants had thought of making it his own.")

The idea of the sleeping car, however, was sound and many men were pondering it. In the latter part of the 1850 decade at least three of them got down to actual work. It matters little who was first, for in the end it was George Pullman who came to build and operate the sleeping cars of the nation.

In 1858 the depot master of the New York Central station at Palatine Bridge, New York, went to Commodore Vanderbilt with designs of a sleeping car. He was Webster Wagner, a former wagonmaker, born in 1817. The plans looked good to the Commodore and he aided Wagner with money to build four cars. They were well made, and had a single tier of berths, and bedding closets at each end of the car. They were put into use on the Central immediately and within a few months were extremely popular, even though Wagner did have a time of it to get his patrons to take off at least their boots before they retired.

Now Wagner, still aided by Vanderbilt, organized the New York Central Sleeping Car Company to build and operate cars exclusively for that road. In 1865 Wagner evolved a drawing-room car—a sort of parlor car—that was dolled up fit to kill with mirrors, polished woods, fine upholstery. This too was a quick success, and now Wagner reorganized to become the Wagner Palace Car Company, out of which he and his associates made fortunes, though not without tangling with George Pullman, of which more later.

While Wagner was getting under way, G. B. Gates, an official of the Lake Shore Railroad, began to make his own sleepers for use on the Lake Shore. In 1869 when the Lake

Shore was taken over by the New York Central, Wagner absorbed the Gates Sleeping Car Company.

Meanwhile, too, Edward Collings Knight, who already had made his pile in sugar and other ventures, thought up a sleeping car and was presently building them for the Baltimore & Ohio and the Camden & Amboy roads. Knight's sleepers, naturally known to all punsters as "Knights," were even more elegant than those made by Wagner. Knight apparently built the best car he could conceive of, using only the finest materials. His cars had berths only on one side, and were three high, two of them double-berths, one single-berth.

Then came T. T. Woodruff, master car builder of the Terre Haute & Alton, who built a series of sleepers that had twelve sections, six on a side; and incorporated a car building company capitalized at $100,000. A little later, and at the unlikely spot of Bangor, Maine, a short-lived concern called the Flower Sleeping Car Company was formed and began putting out a car with the seats down the middle, thus leaving an aisle on each side. In this type of car two berths could be made up into a double bed, if wanted, and one of the claims made for the Flower car was that there was a much freer circulation of air than in other cars.

And now came the celebrated, or at least notorious, Colonel William D'Alton Mann, to design, at first only for the European trade, then for American lines also, the elegant and ingenious Mann's Boudoir Car. It was Mann who really gave Europe the sleeper, and he organized the Compagnie Internationale des Wagons-Lits to supply the demand for them. The Mann job was divided into compartments, or boudoirs as that esthete liked to call them, each entered directly from the side, and "connected by a private door permitting the passage of the attendant to and through the several compartments." Each compartment contained four seats, which by night could be made into beds, although the Mann Boudoirs designed for and operated in the United States had compartments for two persons. They were pretty elegant, too, but their smaller passenger capacity called for a higher rate per passenger than was charged in other sleepers.

"Knights" or "Palace cars" or "Boudoirs," it was all the same to George Mortimer Pullman, the genius of the bed on wheels, who was to take over or break all of his competitors inside of thirty years.

When Pullman arrived in Chicago in 1855 he was twenty-four years old. . . . Like many another man of the period, as we have seen, Pullman had been giving thought to a sleeping car. He was now in a city that fully intended, quite consciously, to become the railroad center of the United States. Many lines already were branching out from the foot of the lake—the Illinois Central, the Burlington, the Chicago & North Western, the Alton. To the Chicago & Alton went young Pullman with his sleeping-car idea. Mildly interested, that road gave him two day coaches which constituted exactly one sixth of the road's rolling stock and told him to see what he could do with them, with his own money, of course.

The two coaches that were to become the first Pullman cars were forty-four feet long, flat-roofed, with the roof a little more than six feet from the floor of the car. There were fourteen windows to a side, each window containing but one pane of glass and that one foot square. Pullman hired Leonard Seibert, a mechanic of the Alton road, to help him remodel the cars during the summer of 1858. Seibert recalled in later years, when he had become something of a historical character by reason of his work on the first Pullmans, that he and Pullman went ahead with no blueprints or drawn plans of any sort. Pullman outlined his ideas, the two men made measurements, cut material to fit, then put the pieces together.

Young Pullman's idea of what constituted a bed may be gleaned by knowing that he and Seibert put ten sleeping sections into each of the cars, plus a linen locker and two wash-rooms, which must have left the bunks little if any more than six feet in length. Pullman wanted to use hickory for the seats and berths, but had to accept cherry wood instead. But into these two cars went Pullman's own idea of an upper berth that could be closed when not in use and also serve to hold the bedding for both upper and lower beds; it was here that Pullman made his first great contribution to the sleeping car.

The upper berth that disappeared during the day was really a radical innovation, brilliant and practical compared to other sleeping cars of the time the bunks of which were permanently placed. But not yet had Pullman arrived at his hinged upper berth. In these first two Pullmans iron rods ran from floor to ceiling. The upper berth was suspended from the ceiling by ropes and pulleys attached to each of the four corners. During the day the berth was pulled up snug to the roof, and by night was let down about halfway between roof and floor. Curtains were used in front and between the berths. The cars had a wood stove at each end. Lighting was still by candle. There were blankets and pillows, but no sheets. . . .

The first month found business just so-so; but it started to pick up and within a short time the two Pullmans were proving so popular on the Chicago & Alton that a third car was converted. The idea did not spread, however, and George Pullman dropped the scheme and went to Colorado, scene of a mining boom, where for the next four years he conducted a store and continued to work on plans for a better sleeping car. He saved his money and in 1863 returned to Chicago with the one idea of making a sleeping car that would be worthy the name.

Taking a boyhood friend, Ben Field of Albion, New York, into a partnership, Pullman and Field applied for and in 1864 were granted two patents, one for the hinged upper berth (No. 42,182), one for hinging the back and seat cushions so that the back could be placed on the seat and the seat cushion extended to meet that of the opposite seat (No. 49,992). Both devices remain unchanged in principle to this day.

Now, indeed, George Pullman had what was needed, but if he had not also possessed great staying powers and salesmanship approaching genius, he might well have given up. It was to be hard going for a while, or until the death of President Lincoln dropped into Pullman's lap a wondrous opportunity of which Pullman made the most. First, of course, Pullman & Field had to incorporate the new ideas into material form. In a shed belonging to the Alton Railroad, on the site now occupied by the Union Station in Chicago, Pullman and Field with artisans took almost a year to build the finest sleeping car ever seen up to that time. Fully equipped, it cost Pullman and his partner all of their capital, or a little more than twenty thousand dollars.

Up to the building of this sleeper, which was named the *Pioneer,* not more than $5,000 had ever been expended on a railway car of any kind. To begin with, the *Pioneer* was a foot wider and two and one-half feet higher than any other car then in service. It rested on improved trucks with springs reinforced by blocks of solid rubber. Every bit of space was utilized, and no iron rods from floor to ceiling marred the beauty of the interior; those upper berth hinges worked to perfection, making by day a clear, uncluttered view from end to end. . . .

The woodwork, the upholstery, and the hangings were magnificent. Much hand carving went into the seats and panels. There was a plush carpet, many mirrors. At one stride, said a historian of the company, an advance of fifty years had been effected.

Whether or not George Pullman knew that the dimensions of his *Pioneer* were too large to permit its passage through many of the stations and bridges of the Chicago & Alton, or of any other railroad of the day for that matter, is not now known. Quite probably he did, and if he did, he must have had a deep faith indeed in his new sleeping car to believe that railroads would change their depot platforms and their bridges just for the sake of drawing it over their lines.

Tradition has it that Mrs. Lincoln, on a visit to Illinois early in 1865, saw and inspected Mr. Pullman's *Pioneer,* and was enchanted. She did not forget its beauty, and when the funeral train to carry the President from Washington to Springfield was being prepared, the widow is said to have requested that the *Pioneer* be attached to it at Chicago for her own use on the remainder of the journey. The request of a President's widow is not to be refused, and the Chicago & Alton, over whose tracks the train would proceed to Springfield, set crews to work hurriedly narrowing the platforms of their way stations and widening the sides of their bridges. . . .

The Alton's line was ready to take the funeral train, couple on the *Pioneer* and proceed to the end of the journey. On May 2nd it pulled out of Chicago under special orders the like of which had not been seen before nor since. The Alton's tracks were, of course, cleared. A pilot engine ran ten minutes ahead of the train, and the pilot could not pass any station unless a white flag by day, or red and white lanterns at night, were displayed. All telegraph stations were kept open continuously. A guard armed with flag and lantern stood at each crossing. The train slowed down as it passed every station, no matter how unimportant, and always the engine's bell was tolled. It tolled through Fort Wayne Junction, through Bridgeport, Summit, Joy's, Lemont, Lockport, Joliet, Stewart's Grove, and finally through Sherman, Sangamon and into Springfield.

Whether or not tradition is right in attributing the quick success of Pullman's new and elegant sleeping car to the whim of Mrs. Lincoln is of little moment, but from this time forward there was no doubt but that George Mortimer Pullman had an idea and ability to be reckoned with. Not long after the Lincoln train, General U. S. Grant rode the Pullman *Pioneer* from Detroit to his old home of Galena, and the Chicago & North Western made the depot platform and the bridge alterations necessary for its passage.

By this time Pullman had engaged a small crew of expert workmen and had set them to building more cars like the *Pioneer*. And presently the rising young industrialist proposed to the Chicago & Alton, which had given him his first and to date only encouragement, that he build and operate sleeping cars for them. The company liked the idea and in this agreement was the genesis of the whole Pullman business.

Pullman's *Pioneer* had cost $20,000 to build. His second, third and perhaps a dozen more cost $24,000 each. They were by far the finest things on wheels in the United States and Pullman intended the public should pay more for riding in them than in the common variety of sleepers. Organizing the Pullman

Palace Car Company in 1867, he placed several of his cars on the Michigan Central and charged 50 cents more per night than the Central charged in its own sleepers. There was no argument. The public was glad to pay the premium, and the other sleepers went begging. Pullman put other cars on the Burlington, then on the Great Western (Grand Trunk). He established his works for a time in Palmyra, New York, but soon moved to Detroit, which for the next decade was the home of the Pullman Palace Cars.

In 1867, too, Pullman made and tried out on the Great Western what he called a Hotel Car. This was a combination sleeping and eating car—berths, with a kitchen in one end of the car, and removable tables set between the seats at mealtimes. This may not have been the first car in which meals were cooked for passengers, but it was unquestionably the finest, for Pullman would have nothing shoddy. Pullman was always an excellent publicist, and this first hotel car was introduced with fanfare and an excursion from Chicago to New York, taking seven days for the trip. Loaded with notables, and marking inauguration of a standard-gauge track between the two big cities that permitted the same cars to pass over the entire trackage, it was heralded as a great event. Pullman sleepers were in the train too, you may be sure, and the party made stops all along the way. Newspapers made much of it, even printing the menu of the hotel car, which, incidentally, offered sugar-cured ham at 40 cents, beefsteak with potatoes at 60 cents, a welsh rarebit at half a dollar.

The hotel-car idea was half way to the diner, and a year later Pullman himself designed his first diner which he named *Delmonico*, after the eminent restaurateur, and put into service on the Chicago & Alton, the guinea-pig route for all of Pullman's experiments. The dining car caught on quickly. Pullman built and also operated diners on a number of lines, while for others he simply built the cars and left them to the individual lines to operate.

Even with high prices of food, and waiters subsidized by the public with tips, few if any railroads ever made money on their dining cars. The opposite has rather been the case. Many a road, faced with strong competition for passengers, has sought to attract trade by serving excellent meals at comparatively low rates. And in 1946, one road, the Pere Marquette, announced that on June 10th it would take an extraordinary, almost a revolutionary step; on that day it would prohibit tipping in its dining cars. "No dagger glances from waiters will follow this step," said a Pere Marquette announcement, "since the company has arranged to compensate workers for any loss incurred."

In 1869 the plains, the mountains, and the Great American Desert were spanned by rails. Pullman was ready for the opportunity, and at once he set his men to building a whole train of special hotel, drawing-room, and sleeping cars, more magnificent even than anything he had conceived before, and at the same time promoted the idea of a first transcontinental trip by steam train, in the same cars, without change, from Boston to San Francisco. The trip was made in 1870, and it was no less than a stroke of genius on Pullman's part. When it was done, Pullman was perhaps the foremost industrial name in the United States, and railroads tumbled over themselves to get contracts with Mr. Pullman to operate his wondrous cars on their lines. Even the Pennsylvania, which had made considerable effort with its own sleeping and dining cars, abandoned its service and came to Pullman.

One should not lose sight of the fact that Pullman did not offer only fine cars to the railroads. His cars, indeed, were the simplest part of the deal. Pullman undertook to operate them, and it was in this department that he revealed even more ability than in his manufacture. There were no precedents to go on. George Pullman had to lay his plans as he went along, then to change them by the trial-and-error method, always costly but usually sure. Slowly he evolved the conception of a system by which passengers might be carried in comfort to almost any part of the nation in cars of uniform construction, equipped for day and night travel, and served and protected by trained employees of Pullman, not of the railroads, whose sole function was to provide for the passenger's safety, comfort, and convenience. . . .

Business of the Pullman Palace Car Company continued to increase through bad years and good, and in 1881 Pullman built a feudal and what many contemporaries held to be the finest "company town" in the country. This was Pullman, on the outskirts of Chicago [now part of Chicago] which for sixteen years continued to be a separate municipality. That Pullman's rents were too high, the public services too costly, and the wages too low, was made all too apparent in 1894 and after, when a strike and an investigation took the headlines of the nation. [Called by the independent American Railway Union under Eugene V. Debs—frequent Socialist candidate for President of the United States—it began with a boycott on servicing Pullman cars, and within weeks had tied up every Middle Western railroad. Attorney General Richard Olney of the United States had 3,400 men sworn in as special deputies to keep trains running and bloody violence resulted in Pullman and elsewhere. At the request of the railroad associations, and over the fervent protests of Governor John Peter Altgeld of Illinois, President Grover Cleveland sent troops to restore order, safeguard the mails, and protect interstate commerce. A Federal court then issued an injunction under the Sherman Antitrust Act forbidding interference with the operation of the mails or interstate commerce. Debs was jailed for contempt of this injunction and the strike was smashed. A writ of habeas corpus to free Debs was denied by the Supreme Court, not on the Sherman Act, but on the broader ground that the relations of the Federal Government to interstate commerce and transportation of the mails authorized the use of the injunction to prevent forcible obstruction.—Ed.]

George Pullman believed in fine cars and also in monopoly. When a competitor showed himself troublesome, Pullman either bought him out, at Pullman's price, or broke him. Knight, Woodruff, Flower, Mann, they all went down before Pullman; and in 1881 Pullman went after the Wagner company, charging infringement of patents to the tune of one million dollars; and again in 1888 he sued Wagner for infringement of patent on the vestibule just put into use by Pullman. Court battles in both cases were extensive. Wagner was probably in the wrong, or at least so the courts found, and Pullman presently took over the last of his competitors.

TWO NOONS ON SUNDAY [5]

There are persons now living who recall when railway operations were in a state of confusion due to lack of a uniform time standard. Prior to adoption of Standard Time the only "time" that existed in this country was local time. Commonly called "sun-time," local time was based upon transit of the sun across the meridian. It varied in the latitude of Boston, Chicago, and Salt Lake City approximately one minute for every thirteen miles, or one second for every 1,140 feet of longitude. In Washington, D.C., there is a difference of 7 seconds between sun-time at the Capitol Dome and sun-time at the Lincoln Memorial. Sun-time at the eastern and western extremes of Chicago differs by about 67 seconds. It differs about 30 seconds between the two ends of the San Francisco-Oakland Bridge. . . .

True sun time was never observed at all points in the country. To have done so would have led to unending confusion because the longitudinal variation is constant. . . . But numerous cities and towns adopted a time standard based upon mean local sun-time at city hall or other designated location. Many another city or town adopted the time standard of one of its railroads or of the principal city in its area. Each railroad adopted the time standard of its home city or of some important city on its lines. . . . The Baltimore & Ohio used Baltimore time for trains running out of Baltimore, Columbus time for trains in Ohio, Vincennes time for trains running west of Cincinnati. Some of its trains ran under New York time, Philadelphia time and Chicago time. The Michigan Central operated on Detroit time. . . . When it was noon in Chicago it was 12:31 in Pittsburgh; 12:24 in Cleveland; 12:17 in Toledo; 12:13 in Cincinnati; 12:09 in Louisville; 12:07 in Indianapolis; 11:50 in St. Louis; 11:48 in Dubuque; 11:39 in St. Paul, and 11:27 in Omaha. . . . In the

[5] From *The Day of Two Noons*, booklet. Association of American Railroads. Transportation Building. Washington 6, D.C. '59. p 4-19. Reprinted by permission.

railroad station in Buffalo, there were three clocks—one set to New York time, by which the New York Central operated; one set to Columbus time, by which the Lake Shore and Michigan Southern and other railroads operated; the other set to local Buffalo time. . . . In Kansas City leading jewelers had their own "standard times," and no two standards agreed. Sometimes the range was as much as twenty minutes. Each jeweler took his own readings. He had customers who set their watches by his regulator and were willing to wager on the correctness of his time. According to one account, "the people of Kansas City never did have accurate information on the arrival and departure of trains, except such as was gained by going to the edge of the hill and looking down on the railway station.". . .

Proposals for a uniform time system were not new. As early as 1828, Sir John Herschel was urging standardization of time in England. On December 6, 1848, partly as a result of his efforts, Greenwich mean time became the standard time of England, Scotland and Wales. One of the earliest advocates of time standardization in the United States was Professor Charles F. Dowd, principal of Temple Grove Ladies' Seminary, at Saratoga Springs, New York. Professor Dowd discussed the need for standardization with a committee of six railway superintendents attending a convention in New York in October 1869. They expressed a desire to see his plan worked out in detail. In a pamphlet published the following year, Professor Dowd presented his hourly-zone plan of standardization, based on Washington time and unvarying longitudinal divisions fifteen degrees apart.

Meanwhile, others were advocating time standardization in one form or another. The *Railroad Gazette* for April 2, 1870, carried an editorial, "Time for the Continent," proposing a standard time for the entire nation. During the 1870's, Professor Benjamin Pierce of Harvard College suggested an "hour-difference" time plan; Sir Sanford Fleming, chief engineer of the Government Railways of Canada, proposed a twenty-four-hour time standard. Dr. Cleveland Abbe, of the United States Signal Service, and Dr. Thomas Hill, president of Harvard College, each advanced plans for some form of standard time for the nation. Like Mark Twain's observation that there had been a great deal of talk about the weather but nothing had ever been done about it, nothing ever came of these proposals until the railroads took the matter in hand.

Railroads Adopt Standard Time

The railroad movement may be said to have had its beginning in May 1872, when an association of railroad superintendents . . . held its first meeting at the old Southern Hotel in St. Louis. At this meeting, called to arrange summer passenger train schedules, a permanent organization was formed which became successively the Time-Table Convention, the General Time Convention, the American Railway Association, and, finally, the Association of American Railroads.

For many years the secretary of the General Time Convention and the American Railway Association was William F. Allen, managing editor of the *Official Guide of the Railways*. In his capacity as Secretary of the General Time Convention, Allen worked unceasingly for the adoption of Standard Time. In the waiting room of Union Station, in Washington, there is a large bronze tablet which gives Allen the credit due him for his part in that very important achievement. Possibly another tablet would be appropriate—this one on the site of the once-famous old Grand Pacific Hotel, in Chicago—to commemorate the General Time Convention of October 11, 1883, which definitely adopted Standard Time.

The plan there adopted provided for five time zones—one, to be known as Intercolonial Time, in the Eastern provinces of Canada, and four in the United States, to be known as Eastern, Central, Mountain and Pacific times. The four United States zones were based upon mean sun-time on the 75th, 90th, 105th and 120th meridians west of Greenwich. These four meridians are approximately on the longitudes of Philadelphia, Memphis, Denver and Fresno. Having voted overwhelmingly to adopt the plan, the convention, through Secretary Allen, issued a notice, directing that all railway clocks governing train operation be set to the new standard at exactly 12 o'clock noon, Sunday, November 18, 1883.

Sunday was selected because fewer trains were in operation at that time and the change could be made with minimum inconvenience and maximum safety. Detailed instructions and recommendations were issued, giving the exact changes necessary for the many railroad companies to adjust their clocks and watches to the new standard, and similar information was furnished public officials of cities throughout the country. It was realized that success of the plan would depend largely upon co-operation of cities and towns in adopting the new time locally, and this was stressed by the General Time Convention and by railway publications. Newspapers and local public officials enthusiastically approved the change, and only scattered opposition was encountered.

November 18, 1883, was called *"the day of two noons."* In the eastern part of each time zone there was a noon based upon sun-time; then clocks and watches were set back from one to thirty minutes to the new Standard Time, so that there was another noon when Standard Time in the community reached 12:00 o'clock. . . . Commenting on the annoyance caused by the change, one newspaper editor said:

The change in time may be annoying to some, but those who are so annoyed should console themselves with the reflection that there is in the Fiji Islands a house which is so divided by the 180th degree of longitude that when it is Sunday in the parlor it is Monday in the kitchen.

A St. Louis newspaper facetiously remarked that it wouldn't make much difference whether some of the western cities, like North Platte and Dodge City, used Central Time or Mountain Time "except to a man who was about to be hanged." Said the editor, "He will be good for another hour of life if he can induce the sheriff to stage the act by Mountain instead of Central Time."

Many legal complications resulted from the changes in time. An interesting case, reported from Iowa, involved the question of whether a fire insurance policy which expired on a certain day should be governed by solar or Standard Time. If sun-time governed, the policy was in force when the fire broke out; but if Standard Time governed, then the policy ceased to be in force $2\frac{1}{2}$ minutes before the fire started. The Supreme Court held that the presumption was that the parties to the contract intended sun-time and decided in favor of the policyholder.

There were many amusing incidents and a few slight hitches in changing from local to Standard Time. For instance, the mayor of Bangor, Maine, refused to recognize the new time on the ground that it was unconstitutional. He even threatened to have the police prevent the churches from ringing their bells on the new time, but popular feeling ran against him and he did not carry out his threat. However, he continued to display the courage of his convictions, and Standard vs. Sun-Time became a first rate political issue in Bangor. The City Council voted for Standard Time; the mayor promptly vetoed the order, declaring that no one had power "to change one of the immutable laws of God."

While most of the clergy endorsed Standard Time, one Boston preacher opposed it on the ground that it was "a lie."

There were many persons who favored some sort of standard time, but could not agree that the system adopted was best. Some wanted time throughout the United States to be uniform, without any time zones. . . . Others were convinced that a mistake was made in not adopting twenty-four-hour time, thus abolishing the use of A.M. and P.M. The Richmond *Dispatch* strongly advocated twenty-four-hour time, declaring that there was no good reason for not adopting that system and attributing failure to do so to "prejudice." The editorial concluded: "Away with old fogyism about twenty-four-hour time.". . .

Adopted Without Federal Legislation

The method of reckoning time instituted by the railroads in 1883, although adopted and used by the Federal Government and states, cities and towns throughout the country, was put into effect without Federal legislation of any sort. It was not until thirty-five years later—on March 19, 1918, during the first World War—that Congress passed what is known as the Standard Time Act.

The Standard Time Act gave the sanction of the Federal Government to the four-zone system adopted by the railroads and provided for "daylight saving" time to conserve fuel and increase national efficiency. The Interstate Commerce Commission was empowered to define by order the boundaries of each Standard Time zone and to make boundary changes deemed necessary. . . .

Daylight Saving went into effect throughout the country on March 31, 1918, but it proved so unpopular that in the summer of 1919 Congress passed a bill repealing the daylight-saving provision of the Standard Time Act. President Wilson vetoed it, but Congress passed it over his veto, and national daylight-saving ended in October 1919.

During the Second World War, Congress provided for year-round daylight saving time throughout the country to conserve fuel and electrical energy in the national emergency. Effective February 9, 1942, this legislation simply put the country ahead an hour without disturbing the four-zone Standard Time system. It was a great improvement over the hodge-podge of "daylight saving" systems superimposed upon the Standard Time system. The provisions of this act were repealed effective September 30, 1945, after cessation of hostilities. Since then, state and local governments have decided for themselves whether to go by Standard Time or daylight-saving time during the summer months.

WHEN TRAINS WERE REALLY TRAINS [6]

Not long ago, as our Pullman was being moved through the Chicago yards, I looked out the rear door and saw racing along, over to my left, a great steam locomotive of the kind called, I believe, a 4-8-4-wheeler, just the big handsome engine and its tender, a cloud of smoke drifting back from its smokestack, its driving rods going like mad. It seemed to me the perfect picture of power on the move. The way it affected me . . . made me realize how scarce they have become, how great the danger that

[6] From article by Oliver La Farge, anthropologist, ethnologist, and 1929 Pulitzer Prize winner for his novel *Laughing Boy. The Reporter.* 21:35-7. O. 1, '59. Copyright © 1959 by Oliver La Farge. Reprinted by permission of Oliver La Farge and *The Reporter.*

we are about to lose the last of a feature of America that is, to my mind, quite as worth saving as the redwoods. . . .

In the 1920's there was still plenty of ruggedness to transcontinental train travel. Without air conditioning, windows were opened and dust and smoke blew in. Before tunnels, everything had to be shut tight and we sweltered. A young man, traveling cheap, took trains that made meal stops, where he encountered the now legendary girls of the Harvey station restaurants. There were unexpected, unexplained waits in the middle of nowhere, in prairie, desert, or mountains, when you could feel the silence and the space close in (that sounds like a contradiction in terms, but it is what happens, for in the West, emptiness is a thing), and sometimes hear a bird, or a calf calling in the distance, to bring home to you fully the din in which you had been traveling. Noise, smoke, and motion—in them was safety, the assurance that these two thin lines of steel with wilderness on either hand really would lead you to your destination and the haunts of men. When motion ceased and all was quiet, you were not so sure. All in all, you could imagine that you shared something with the pioneers of the covered wagons, and of those quaint, fabulous trains with the tall, bulbous smokestacks and the coal stoves in the parlor cars of an earlier age. Riding streamliners today behind thin-voiced Diesels, I realize that in fact we did have more in common with those old-timers than we realized.

Trains in the night crossing the wide nation, the stops, the glimpses of lanterns and snatches of voices, the whistle reaching out over the curve of the world, have been more than adequately described. (I doubt that Thomas Wolfe would have written as he did of trains had he ridden only on the streamliners of today.) I shall not add to the descriptions; I want to use the nighttime train simply to bring us back fully to my subject, the engines, the smoke-and-steam-breathing, fire-carrying, well-voiced creatures. The train of cars is inanimate. Barring the allowance we must make for everyone's feeling about cabooses, it is just the engine's load; disconnect it, and it has no character. The tender is the engine's faithful follower and necessary helper. What gives the whole assemblage life is the engine, and as you lay in your berth at night, even after air conditioning had sealed the windows, this was made unforgettably manifest in the ritual drumming of the start after each stop, the first heavy puffs, the very choo-choo, the old chant of "I think I can, I think I can . . ." and so on to the full triumphant rush of the fast beat in which the single strokes were almost, but not quite, blended into a continuous roar.

Always, the romance comes back to the steam engine, one of the two most animate things man ever made, the other being the sailing ship. In these engines there was a wonderful continuity. In 1829, our first locomotive, imported from England, made a run in the United States. It was, comparatively, a feeble thing. The locomotives grew up almost exactly in step with the opening of the West. Conestoga wagons had been used in Pennsylvania for freighting some seventy-five years earlier, but the westward-venturing prairie schooner was the contemporary and complement of the steam locomotive. Between the two, the continent was occupied and its extremes tied together; then the work of the schooners ended, while that of the engines had hardly begun. It was they that made possible the internal commerce without which the West would never have been worth really populating. Without the steam trains, Texans would still be slaughtering gaunt longhorns and shipping only the hides; without the steam trains, California oranges and Oregon apples would still be strictly for local consumption.

The great work was done by the nearest thing to a real dragon the world has known since the age of dinosaurs—but there were no men around to fear and admire the dinosaurs, and at their fearsome best they were cold beasts. The engines were lovable, docile, useful dragons, adored by generations of children and by those children grown up. It is all one lineage, from that first specimen to the giants that we rode behind until just the other day.

No wonder that songs and tales gathered around them—"Casey Jones," "The Wreck of the Old 97." No wonder that, even today, children's books and toys present the steam engines, and a delightful children's record, "Sparky and the Talking Train," features one. The grownups, the book and record makers, the designers of toys, the buyers of gifts, cannot quite bring themselves to admit that this inheritance has all but gone. The children first learn "choo-choo," one way or another, but then one day they come up with the observed fact that the noise trains make is "chick-a-chick," and we are soon forced out of our memories. In only a few places now in our country can a choo-choo be seen; in its place we have a chick-a-chick, which blows a whistle that makes a piddling sound, scientifically calculated for audibility and about as impressive as the cry of a medium-sized cat.

We are in immediate danger of losing forever a genus of creatures as well worth saving, I repeat, as the redwoods or the whooping cranes. I am a writer, not an organizer, so I am writing this piece in the hope of stirring up others, perhaps someone who does know how to organize and get things done, to act to save a few steam locomotives for their children and for themselves. A number of cities at this time are arranging or have already arranged to have an iron horse mounted on a pedestal, little more than a museum exhibit of a dead dragon. Surely it would be worthwhile to save a few live ones, to get the railroads to come together on an arrangement for running a few steam trains in some sort of rotating arrangement about the country.

When the steam train arrived, schools would let out, you may be sure. Or if they did not, innumerable parents and uncles would bring the small fry and gladly pay, for the young and for themselves, to take even a short ride once more behind a choo-choo and to stand on the platform and admire it.

II. PEOPLE AND PLACES

EDITOR'S INTRODUCTION

"If we have done anything wrong," said J. P. Morgan to Theodore Roosevelt in 1903, "send your man to my man and they can fix it up." The man that the elder Morgan wanted the President of the United States to send calling on his lawyer was the Attorney General of the United States and the little matter he thought the two eminent counsel could fix up between them was an antitrust suit being brought by the government against the Northern Securities Company. The Northern Securities Company was a holding company that controlled the Great Northern, the Northern Pacific, and the Chicago, Burlington & Quincy railroads, and in 1904 it was duly dissolved by the Supreme Court under the Sherman Antitrust Act, but its passing marked more than another victory in Roosevelt's "trust-busting" campaign. It marked the end of an era in which the railroads and their bankers could conduct their business with an arrogance that is still unique in the corporate annals of the land. Memories of that arrogance, best expressed and best remembered in William H. Vanderbilt's classic "The public be damned," still linger in the national consciousness to aggravate the many ills that now beset the railroads, though all the sinning was not on one side.

Two groups were early, loud, and frequently effective in their antagonism to the railroads. These were the clergy and the farmers. (There was also a third—legislators who would introduce railroad harassing bills into state legislatures for the sole purpose of being bought off—but this group was so specialized as to be without sociological significance.) The clergy, while clamorous for free passes (they still ride half-fare), attacked the railroads as Sabbath-breakers. Most were probably sincere, feeling that railway workers should have Sunday as a day of rest, but there is reason to suspect that many found that the pleasure of "riding the cars" on a Sunday outing was cutting church attendance and they fought the new distraction through various Sabbath Committees and Lord's Day Alliances. Few met the success of the one in Altoona, Pennsylvania, which persuaded the city fathers to prohibit the movement of trains on Sunday. Altoona, as a local minister pointed out, became "one city where locomotives keep the Sabbath" and any train caught there at midnight Saturday simply stayed there until Monday. The railroads, supported by the public, generally ignored the religious threat or fought it with free passes, the purchase of state legislators, or magnificent hypocrisy. "Persons purchasing tickets for Sunday trains," ran an 1850 notice in the Table of Arrangements (timetables) of an ancestor of the Boston & Maine, "will be required to sign a pledge they will use the tickets for no other purpose than attending church."

Opposition by the clergy had pretty much disappeared by 1870 but the falling torch was grasped by another and more justified opponent, the farmers. Their enmity dated almost from the first rail, for they claimed with considerable truth that steam locomotives frightened their horses, set fire to their crops, and sprayed their wives' washing with soot, but their antagonism became a great deal more purposeful in 1867 with the founding of the National Grange of the Patrons of Husbandry. Founded as a social organization for farmers and their wives it soon took on political overtones and its political philosophy was simple. "The soil is the source from whence we derive all that constitutes wealth," said the prospectus of the order, so it naturally followed that anyone who denied his full share of that wealth to the tiller of the soil should be enjoined by law. To the Grange, quite justifiably, the railroads were the chief offenders against the farmers; and against the railroads the organized farmers—feeling their political oats for the first time—pushed hundreds of so-called "granger laws" through state legislatures. Most of these laws ranged from the ill-advised to the ridiculous and many were either repealed before they were effective or ignored as impractical. But those against arbitrary, capricious, or excessive freight and passenger rates were sustained by the

Supreme Court in a number of decisions which held that while the railroads were privately owned they were "clothed with a public interest" that justified their regulation by the states. It was these decisions, bitterly fought by the railroads but almost gracefully acquiesced in once made, that led to the state regulation of carriers, the Interstate Commerce Act of 1887, and the Interstate Commerce Commission.

Once the railroads had been tamed by law the National Grange of the Patrons of Husbandry gradually reverted to its original social purpose and let its more militant members continue the fight against monopolies under such banners as the Farmers' Alliance, the Greenbackers, the Brothers of Freedom, the Cooperative Union of America, and the Populist Party. None of these ever accomplished the lasting good that was achieved by the Grange in fathering the ICC, for although the Commission has been criticized and abused by both public and carriers, it has proved to be one of the most useful and needed controls in our system of government. The Interstate Commerce Act was the first major regulatory legislation of the Federal Government and, with the Interstate Commerce Commission, it established the pattern for almost all subsequent regulation of business: the delegation of power to a small and wieldy commission of competent, experienced, and informed administrators. In this Commission, as the articles in this section make abundantly clear, lies the best hope for a solution to the myriad problems that face the railroads in a changing land with a changing people and a changing economy.

TRANSPORTATION'S THREE-WAY SNARL [1]

Our national transportation system is in . . . a mess. That is a flat statement of fact, and it is true whether you look up at our great airliners in the sky, or down at our more prosaic vehicles on the ground. It is true of every pathway we travel, and something has to be done about it soon.

[1] From "Unsnarling Traffic on the Roads, Rails, and Airways," article by John I. Snyder, Jr., president of United States Industries, Inc. *Harper's Magazine.* 217:31-6. N. '58. Reprinted by permission.

In the sky, disasters are piling up, and airline executives—caught in a dilemma beyond their total control—can hardly sleep nights for the cold fear of wondering where and when tragedy will strike next. . . . On the ground, the railroads are just as badly off, and railroad executives are not sleeping well either. Their nightmare is not death; it is financial collapse. The truth is that as things stand now our railroads—vital to our national welfare—are plunging downhill toward insolvency, and very little has been done about it. On another part of the ground, there is still another dilemma—the one we all know best: our highways are too crowded and they're getting more so all the time.

That, in brief, is our dismal transportation picture. Individually, each of the messes—in the air, on the rails, and on the highways—is staggering in its own very complex terms; and up to now our nation's transportation experts have tended to deal with each one separately.

Thus Congress moves to help the rails, and Senator George Smathers says that without some such action "catastrophe" will strike and the railroads will "go under." Simultaneously we launch our huge new Federal Highway Program. At the same time the Civil Aeronautics Administration, properly alarmed about recent midair collisions, sets up a new controlled Super Skyways Plan—admitting, however, that the plan cannot assure "absolute safety" in the air. And President Eisenhower backed the establishment of the new Federal Aviation Agency—a sort of consolidation of the CAA and the Airways Modernization Board.

These surely are urgently needed measures, and Congress, in the face of public impatience, is acting quickly on most of them. Yet many of us must begin to wonder how we got into such trouble on so many fronts in the first place, and whether what we're doing about it now is enough.

In my opinion what we're doing is good, but it is not enough. I believe that up to now we have made one fundamental mistake in all our transportation planning—we have consistently failed to recognize that basic problems have begun to emerge which are common to *all* forms of transport, and which must be solved together. We have carefully kept our air-lane, railroad, and highway planners far apart from each other, in separate, air-tight rooms. And no one to date has asked the ultimate question, which is this: *How does each means of transportation fit, properly, into an over-all transportation pattern which is broad enough to contain and support them all—and within which each can help its competitors?*

The question must be faced, and it *can* be answered. The plain fact is that such a pattern exists—all we have to do is find it.

Too Many Planes?

Let us look first at our airways, where the basic problem is safety.

Everyone who reads newspapers knows that the air is not totally safe today. There are too many landings and take-offs at our big airports, and our air lanes are too crowded. Many among us have been in near collisions in recent years and don't even know it.

If this is true today, what of tomorrow, when bigger, faster planes will be flying in greater numbers than ever before? It is well known that we have already started producing a great new fleet of giant jet airliners, huge craft that will move at 600 miles per hour—double the present airliner's average speed. These planes will be so economical to operate that flight in them will cost us, as passengers, nearly a third less than airline flight costs now. As a result, by 1975 three times more civilian passengers will be flying three times more passenger miles than at the present time, and the number of planes in the sky over the United States will have increased from 90,000 to 125,000.

This is doubtless an exciting prospect, but frankly it frightens me. If controlling our air lanes to make them safer has become a monumentally difficult task under present conditions, how can we hope to handle the speed and growth of our jet-age future?

It is true that we are now finally coming to grips with this pressing problem. We are blue-printing a super-plan for an air-control network. Excellent men are involved in this project . . . experts who firmly believe that their network can be established and will probably work.

They may be right, but I remain uneasy, for I believe there are limits to their plan which they have overlooked. These limits are simply the amount of space available in our skies.

To my mind it is strange that these physical limits are seldom, if ever, mentioned. Although we may successfully establish super-highways of the sky—although our jet-age planes may fly along them, under ideal controlled conditions, in solitary (and therefore "safe") blocks of air space—still it seems obvious that as more and more planes take to the sky, we will have to reduce the protective cocoons of space around each plane merely to squeeze them all into our air highway pattern. The moment we begin doing this, the super-highways will not be so safe any more.

Something Has to Give

The truth is that you are and always will be infinitely safer in an uncrowded sky than in a crowded one. The key to the whole safety equation is air traffic density—the number of planes in the sky. This will remain so, it seems to me, no matter how sophisticated our traffic controls may become. And for this reason I submit that *we must try to cut air traffic density wherever we can.*

This notion is extremely simple but, on the basis of what has gone before, it sounds radical. Up to now no expert has suggested it even as a partial solution to the air-safety problem. Everybody seems to assume that all demand for high-speed traffic in this country in future years will be directed *into the air,* and that more and more congestion in the sky is inevitable.

I don't believe this is so. I believe the opposite—that something has to give, and that a large body of air traffic can be taken out of the sky with great benefit for all forms of airborne transport *and for all other forms of transport as well.* Further, I believe that a good substitute for this air traffic is available—at least potentially—on the ground.

Obviously there is much air traffic that we cannot do without. Clearly we must not tamper with military flights (except to try to keep the military's jets under control in our air lanes); nor

should we fiddle with intercontinental and transcontinental flights
—by every yardstick of speed and economy they clearly belong
where they are. Local and general aviation is mostly centered
around scattered minor airports and doesn't often even come
close to the major air routes, so we can leave it alone so long as
it is well controlled.

There is another segment of air traffic, however, which doesn't
make sense from any point of view—that which the airlines call
"low priority" or short-distance travel. To begin with, those of
us who travel from 100 to 500 miles by air are not profitable
passengers for the airlines—they actually lose money on short-
haul business (unless they have a feeder line subsidy from the
government).

Even more important, short-haul traffic accounts for a surprisingly large share of the congestion in the air. At peak hours
about 80 per cent of all air-carrier movements in Washington,
D.C., about a fifth in Chicago and Los Angeles, and one third in
New York are short-haul—both inbound and outbound. One of
the world's busiest, and therefore most dangerous, air corridors
stretches from Boston to New York to Washington—a short-haul
run.

This situation is sure to worsen unless something radical is
done about it. . . . Estimates [are] that by 1975 our short-distance
flights will have multiplied more than five times, while long-haul
flights, in marked contrast, will have grown by only two-and-a-
half times.

Plainly short-haul air service leaves much to be desired in
every way, and if something has to give to relieve congestion in
the air, this is it.

It can't give quite yet, however. The short-distance traveler is
still with us, demanding to be moved wherever he wants to go
quickly and in comfort. This is his right, and he can enforce it
simply by continuing to use the air lanes until we provide him
with something at least as good on the ground.

Finding the right substitute isn't easy, however. Since we
habitually compartmentalize our transport problems, we are not
accustomed to thinking about how to achieve the most economic

and efficient means for each type of traffic. Now, I think, is a good time to begin, so let us look along the ground—at our highways and our rails—to see if we can find a short-haul replacement.

Paralysis on the Ground

At first glance both are discouraging. If there are too many planes in the sky, there are many more cars on our roads, where congestion has reached a ludicrous peak. Also most of us would probably guess—in spite of our preference for riding in our own cars—that the highways are *not* an economic means of travel, short-haul or long. Your automobile may be convenient and comfortable, but if you have done any cost computations lately you know it is expensive to operate.

The highways themselves, of course, are growing—but at a huge cost. Since 1948, the concrete and asphalt ribbon of our Federal-aid highway system, comprising all main national and state arteries, has increased by 160,000 miles—the equivalent of a fifty-lane super-highway running coast to coast. Our bill for this was $11 billion—a bargain by today's standards. The 41,000 miles of road to be built under the Federal Highway Act of 1956 will involve total expenditures of *$38 billion*—if costs don't rise by the time the roads are finished in 1975.

We are paying for all this in rising tolls and taxes. Still our highway experts say we are running behind, that further sharp rises in highway density are in sight. Meanwhile most of us are driving a lot faster than we used to. Consequently death by automobile, now our No. 1 Killer, is exacting an annual toll roughly one hundred times greater than that of plane and rail accidents combined.

In view of all this, it is clearly silly even to begin to think of shifting our short-haul air traffic from our crowded skies to our more crowded highways. We would merely be moving congestion from one place to another where the danger would be even greater; also it would be too expensive. Solving our highway problem, like solving our air-lane problem, centers on *reducing* traffic—not adding to it.

What, then, of our railroads? Can we find our replacement there?

To many railroad men, the idea that they might take over short-haul traffic from the air lanes would sound so absurd that they would laugh you out of the room if you brought it up. As safety is the chief problem in the air today, so money—or the lack of it—is the unbearable burden of our railroads. And, paradoxically the villain here is again *the short-haul passenger*.

Short-haul passenger traffic has hurt our railroads even more than it is now hurting the airlines. On such eastern roads as the Central and Pennsylvania, short-run trains have racked up tremendous deficits. As a result, road after road has submitted plans to the ICC for relief from the short-haul passenger. Simultaneously the western roads have tried desperately (through Vistadome cars and other lures) to retain their *long-haul* passengers—but without real success so far.

It is a safe bet that neither the eastern nor western roads will win their points. Most long-haul passengers are virtually sure to abandon the rails sooner or later, no matter what the roads do; and there are plenty of good reasons—all founded in the public interest—why no railroad is likely to be permitted to dispense altogether with its short-haul clientele.

Here we have one point on which rails and airlines can agree: no matter how he moves, the short-distance traveler remains unprofitable and unwanted.

A Job for the Daring

Our national railway system must—and will—continue to operate, of course. No airplane can haul iron ore or tow steel beams, and there are thousands of other commodities that can be transported economically only by rail. What is alarming about the railroads' present condition is that another round of bankruptcies might easily lead to governmental ownership and operation—a drastic solution which nobody really wants.

So the task facing our railroad managers is not only to save their roads, but to save them freely and on their own, before the government has to take over. To do this, they will have to

operate not only efficiently, but with great daring and imagination
—for the old railroading concepts just don't seem to work any
more.

Their first big undertaking, it seems to me, should be to woo
the short-haul passenger. He may be a thorny traveler, but I
believe he can be had, and that the prize is worth the game.

There are several good reasons why the railroads should tackle
the short-haul job—and why they can make money doing so, if
they do it right. Even today they can carry traffic between many
of our cities, during peak hours, faster than most of us can
drive the same runs in our private cars. The explanation is that
the railroads already possess the physical characteristics of any
sensible rapid ground-transport system—the rights of way directly
connecting our metropolitan centers. Their terminals are far
better located than any airport can be. Moreover, excellent studies
have shown that a railroad right of way can accommodate twenty
times more people than an express highway lane, and that it costs
only one fifth as much to transport people by rail as by road.

Why then are the railroads losing money on their present
short-haul operations? There is of course no reason why they
should continue to provide us with services at prices below cost—
particularly when their services are so vital.

I think the answer is simply that traditional railroading is too
slow to compete with air travel. It can't provide adequate speeds
with a reasonable factor of safety, and people go out of their
way to avoid it so long as faster, more comfortable transport is
available. Yet the railroads must continue to offer the service.
The financial results of this squeeze have been ruinous.

In view of this, it seems clear to me that if the railroads are
indeed the logical medium to take over the great body of our
short-haul inter-city passenger traffic, *what has to be found and
financed is an entirely new method of carrying such traffic,
quickly, along our railroad rights of way.*

Exactly what the new form of short-haul railroading should
be, I don't pretend to know. Maybe the answer lies in the
exploration of the monorail system, in which cars travel not on
double tracks, but on single steel beams attached to pylons. There

are several varieties of monorail; in some the cars are mounted above the beams, in others they are slung below. In all they move quietly and safely at very high speeds and are capable of rounding steeply banked curves without slowing down.

The monorail originated in Germany, and one has been running in Wuppertal, in the Ruhr, for more than fifty years. In Cologne, Germany, a new model monorail called the ALWEG System has been developed and is on display. In America, we have an experimental monorail on display in Dallas—the early prototype of a system that has been proposed for inter-city service between Fort Worth and Dallas.

But the monorail hasn't really caught on yet. Initial costs of installation are high and have mitigated against its acceptance even in cases where railroads have been willing to donate their rights of way for experimentation. Also the monorail doesn't carry freight—it is a single-purpose system usually intended only for urban passenger traffic.

But the monorail, of course, isn't the only possibility lying at the technological frontier. Dr. A. A. Kucher, Vice President of Engineering at Ford Motor Company, has been working on a "Glideair" vehicle—a high-speed sled which rides on a cushion of air.

Are Deficits Inevitable?

There is the possibility that we can achieve high-speed ground transport with a relatively simple adaptation of historic railroading techniques. The Japanese National Railway has just announced that it is planning to spend more than $500 million in the next six years on a new electrified train designed to ride on broad-gauge, jointless rails embedded in concrete. This train is already billed as the world's fastest; it is expected to travel between 100 and 150 miles per hour and it will make the run from Osaka to Tokyo—a 320-mile stretch—in three hours or less.

The actual form of future high-speed land transport, however, is not the point here. The point is that some such form is needed. Without it, we will probably be forced to accept public authorities as our railroad managers. One such authority is already under consideration in Massachusetts, where a bill has been filed to create an area transportation commission to operate the commuter service around Boston which the New Haven Railroad, by Federal court order, has been permitted to abandon. Under the bill, the authority would lease tracks and the railroad's operating deficit would be borne by Boston and other cities and towns along the way.

But why should we accept passenger deficits when the situation can be remedied by applied research in rapid ground transportation? Why do we avoid such research? All we need is a vehicle that can carry us faster along the ground, from the center of Boston to the center of Washington, say, than a 500-mile-per-hour aircraft can carry us—and this can be done by a safe land carriage moving at only *100 miles per hour!*

Plainly substantial benefits for all transportation would flow from any sensible solution along these lines. Really fast, comfortable, conveniently scheduled short-haul rail service would rejuvenate the roads' sick passenger operations and would place them once again on a profitable basis, for it would not only help them regain the passengers they've lost, but would also generate new and large passenger revenues. Morning and night, the new fast-haul runs might be partially integrated with "commuter" runs. Eventually they might even extend the present outer edges of our normal commuter zones, opening up new areas—as far as one hundred miles beyond city lines—for suburban settlement.

This solution would also ease the congestion in the air. In addition to bringing short-haul air passengers back to the ground, it would enable intercontinental and transcontinental planes to land *not* in crowded air terminals like those in New York, where they usually have to waste time and fuel while waiting their turn in stacks, but in less crowded terminals in cities connected, by fast short-run trains, with the metropolitan centers. Passengers would reach their ultimate destinations as quickly as they do now, if not more so.

In our big cities, finally, bumper-to-bumper road traffic would thin out. We would all think twice before driving even short hauls if we could get there in half the time, and more comfortably, in some other form of transport. The present pressure for costly mid-town parking facilities would be greatly reduced, and far less carbon monoxide would be discharged into our metropolitan atmospheres.

The Long Pull

This is the kind of transportation thinking we badly need today. The project outlined here would be tremendously complex and expensive. Private enterprise—probably the railroad managers—should get it started; but once it is under way the government would have to be very much involved. The necessary capital expenditures should, in fact, be borne by the government.

The truth is that the government is already spending billions on a disconnected patchwork of vast, individual transportation programs. This is ridiculous at the present stage of our technological development and in view of our huge transportation problems. As a nation we can no longer afford unplanned free choice in transportation. We do not live in a limitless world, as we did when we were very young and our frontier was expanding. Space has limitations, in transportation as well as in communications. In communications, we have always allocated channels for radio, television, and telephone signals—failure to do so would have led to chaos on our airwaves. Now the same thing turns out to be true in transportation: we have to treat it as one whole.

What we need first, then, is a group to study it as one whole. This group should consist of trained and expert technicians in all forms of transport; of the dedicated public servants who run government agencies like the CAA and the ICC; of Cabinet members (particularly in Commerce and Interior); and of the civilian leaders who run our railroads, our airlines, our trucks, and our buses, and who build our roads. It should be their assignment to determine what part of the over-all transportation job in this country should be handled by what media—and on what physical and economic terms.

The assignment obviously is a tough one—at least as tough as unification of our Armed Forces—but it is just as important as unification and we can't avoid it any longer. We must have efficient transportation in times of peace and war, and we don't have it now. Therefore the formation of this transportation group should receive highest priority in government and the President should start preparing immediately for it. To begin with, he might well discuss the idea with congressional leaders of both parties who would ultimately have to approve the necessary expenditures. It is also conceivable that . . . [the] governors of New York, New Jersey, and Connecticut—whose states are most deeply embroiled in our national transportation muddle—may want to set up a parallel study group of their own.

Twenty-five years ago, at the depth of the great depression, a group of institutional investors invited Calvin Coolidge, Governor Alfred E. Smith, and Bernard Baruch to help form a National Transportation Committee.

"There is no more important present task," the investors said at that time, "than a thorough and satisfactory solution of the railroad problem, *as an integral part but the most urgent part of the entire transportation problem.*"

We have revolutionized our transportation technology since then, but we still don't have a national transportation policy. We must formulate one now. It is the only way we will ever straighten out our mess and develop a sensible, workable transportation program which will benefit every form of transport and the public as well.

WHAT'S HAPPENED TO THE RAILROADS? [2]

The remedy for the present railroad situation can be summed up in railroad language: get government the hell out of clumsy interference with transportation. . . . But before we can sensibly discuss remedies we must understand what has happened to United States transportation and what the situation is today.

World War I was followed by the era of the internal-combustion engine. This was paralleled by further rapid expansion of the iron and steel industry, with its impact upon

[2] From "What's Wrong with the Railroads?" article by Perry M. Shoemaker, president of the Delaware, Lackawanna & Western railroad and formerly chairman of the transportation subcommittee of the second Hoover Commission on Organization of the Executive Branch of the Government. *Fortune.* 61:118-19+. Reprinted by special permission from the January 1960 issue of *Fortune* magazine. © 1959 by Time Inc.

Great Lakes bulk transportation of raw materials and by the rapid development of pipelines for oil, and later natural gas. The period between the two world wars was one of rapid highway development to keep pace with the manufacturing of pleasure cars and (later) over-the-road trucks. Few toll highways were built, our political conception being one of a socialized intercity highway system paid for by the taxpayer—not without great encouragement from the rubber, petroleum, and automobile industries.

The decade before World War II saw the beginning of airport and airway development, likewise from public funds. This socialization was claimed to be justifiable as public policy toward an infant industry, and was augmented by great operating subsidy payments to most, if not all, of the airlines. The amount of this operating subsidy to major domestic airlines has in recent years declined, with some receiving none directly, but the indirect aids continue, and multiply. As the Congressional Conference Report of August 18, 1959, accompanying H.R. 7978 (and refusing certain additional millions for cargo-aircraft development through the back door of supplemental appropriations), stated so plainly: "Civilian aviation has grown by virtue of the generous subsidy it has received from the government. It is now a giant grown fat by government subsidies and high rate charges."

In the period between the two wars, socialization became firmly entrenched in the maritime industry. Public policy gave both construction and operating subsidies to the American merchant marine to overcome lower foreign-flag labor and material costs. Need for a merchant marine for defense was the primary reason given to justify this development.

The Army Engineers, with much local political encouragement, were quick to accept a philosophy involving tremendous capital investments by the government for inland-waterway facilities for the discriminatory benefit of a relatively few private users.

In World War II, with a shortage of oil and rubber, the basic economic superiority of railroad transportation again became apparent under the pressure of emergency. Soon 90 per cent of the nation's military transportation of freight and 97 per cent of the organized military transportation of passengers was by railroad. In a manner unprecedented in history, the railroads mobilized, and World War II ended with general acclaim for the magnificent job that the railroad industry had done.

In the period since World War II, competition between modes of transportation has become more intense than at any time in the country's history, with inflationary forces particularly helping the relative opportunity for air, highway, and inland-waterway transportation because of their benefit from great capital outlays by the public. The commercial users of these facilities had not been required to make the capital investment in the first place, nor pay for them in the second, with the result that their charges to the public for transportation have been relatively low. To match their prices the railroads, meeting their full costs—including taxes on property—have had an increasing economic problem. The last decade and a half has brought the dieselization of most of the railroad operations in the country, great developments in centralized traffic control, electronic classification yards, and mechanized maintenance and freight handling. All of this self-improvement, averaging more than a billion dollars a year, was made in a period of inflation when traffic volume was declining, and the net result, particularly in the East, has been economic weakening rather than improvement in the position of the railroads. . . .

Political leaders seem to lack understanding of what further socialization means, and threatens, to the nation's transportation system as a whole. Naïve stupidity, however, will not explain the part played by certain bureaucrats looking forward with anticipation to government "take-over" of the railroad industry as the first step to nationalization of transportation.

What does the record show?

The St. Lawrence Seaway had been talked about by the proponents of waterway transportation for at least forty years. Of course, government was to provide the facilities—the channels, the harbors, the dams and locks. This was opposed by the bulk of American business until the turn-about of the steel industry, which came with the development of Labrador ore. Again using the timeworn argument that the St. Lawrence Seaway was necessary for defense, even though it is usable only eight months of the year, the [Eisenhower] Administration was persuaded to embrace the idea. Now the seaway is a reality that is seriously damaging public surface transportation by rail and highway in the whole eastern half of the country.

Public capital has supplied the seaway. Much more public capital is being demanded to deepen the channels and improve the harbors. The September 1959 estimate of N. R. Danielian of the Great Lakes-St. Lawrence Association gives a ten-year requirement of at least half a billion dollars. Tolls for the present seaway, as established this year, are not adequate in themselves to pay for the investment and operation and maintenance costs over a period of fifty years, as generously provided in the statute. And, in addition to all of this, there are new differential operating subsidies to American-flag users of the seaway who commit themselves to serve government-specified routes.

Under the current Administration steady improvement has been made in inland waterways other than the St. Lawrence Seaway. The channels, locks, and navigational aids on the Ohio, Mississippi, Missouri, and Hudson rivers, for instance, are all made available to users of these arteries virtually free of any cost. Small wonder that waterway tonnage is increasing when such an important part of its real cost is coming from the public till.

Pressure on the Administration resulted in its embracing the idea of a super interstate-highway system to enhance, among other things, the interests of the automobile and truck manufacturers, the rubber industry, and the petroleum industry. Nor has the highway-construction industry been uninterested in the development. This new interstate-highway system, too, was supposed to be needed for defense purposes. It, too, was supposed to be paid for by special taxes on users—but the pay-as-you-go principle has been impaired before the program is even off the ground.

Had the interstate-highway system been approached by the Administration and Congress as a toll-road concept, with all users paying on a fair basis as between pleasure cars and trucks, and thus earning full costs currently, the impact upon private-enterprise railroad transportation would have been much less.

The public sponsorship of fine highway facilities, with government maintenance, government policing, government snow removal, government ice sanding, and government signaling, makes it incredibly easy for the bus and truck operators to compete with the railroads, and indeed to have private operators or quasi-private truck operators compete with common-carrier truck transportation. It is not generally realized that two-thirds of the intercity truck transportation is unregulated and consists of exempt trucking (largely of agricultural products or byproducts), private trucking, and "for hire" carriers operating without authorization. . . .

The Dead Hand of 1887

The period since World War II has been characterized by a virtual revolution in distribution practices. The kinds of goods have changed with the rapid development of plastics and light metals and countless advances in technology. Industry today requires fast movement, direct delivery, and much specialized equipment involving great capital investments, such as special-device cars for automobile parts and special gondolas for strip steel. The impact of government help to other forms of transportation, together with inflation, places the railroads in a position where they cannot build up funds to meet such new equipment requirements and otherwise modernize as rapidly as they should. Thus has public policy reacted to endanger critically the survival of railroad transportation as private enterprise.

Despite all of the changes in competition, particularly postwar, there has been but limited modification of the regulation imposed upon the railroad industry in 1887, when the railroads were deemed to have a monopoly of transportation. The Eisenhower Administration showed some awareness of this when, in

1954, it established a Cabinet committee to look into the transportation picture and recommend legislative changes. An extensive study was made by some of the most competent transportation men in the country. . . . For all practical purposes this report was filed away, and the Administration failed to make use of a great opportunity to effect a start toward some coordination and some equality of treatment between the modes of transportation.

It remained for a Democratic Congress in 1958 to hold extensive hearings on "The Deteriorating Railroad Situation," and to produce an incisive report, followed by the Transportation Act of 1958, which made a start toward improving the competitive position of the railroad industry. Freight rates were not to be set by the ICC at a particular level in order to protect the traffic of any other mode of transportation. The 1958 act encouraged all carriers to make rates reflecting their own inherent advantages. The broad exemptions from regulation for highway transportation of agricultural commodities were somewhat modified.

A guaranteed-loan statute was established so that, under rigid standards created to protect the public and subject to investigation by the ICC, a commercial loan to a railroad otherwise without adequate credit would be guaranteed by the Federal Government.

The effect of this legislation is, of course, long range. The improved status of competitive rate making apparently offers great promise. The legislation is not a panacea, but it does represent steps in the direction of modernized regulation and improved opportunity for rail and highway carriers.

Additional aspects of transportation were left for further study by the Congress, and such a study is now in progress by the Senate Interstate and Foreign Commerce Committee. At the request of the President, the Department of Commerce is currently engaged in a long-needed evaluation of Federal transportation policy.

In my judgment the most constructive step that could be taken would be the creation of a Cabinet-level Department of

Transportation. It should not have regulatory powers. It should have the responsibility for integrating all the promotional interests of government in all forms of transportation; for preserving to the public the inherent advantages of each; and for encouraging continuing improvements in transportation.

It does not make sense for the Bureau of Public Roads to be operating in a vacuum in so far as the relationship of its planning to other types of transportation is concerned. It is not sound public administration to have the Army Engineers drafting multimillion-dollar improvement programs for inland waterways in disregard of the economic impact on highway and rail transport, and without evaluation of whether such improvements are needed in the broad public interest of the country as a whole. It is ridiculous for the Maritime Administration to be in the position of blindly approving government subsidy of coastwise, seaway, and intercoastal transportation not only in disregard of, but without knowledge of, its impact upon other transportation systems. It is of questionable public interest for the Civil Aeronautics Board to approve great subsidies to feeder airlines and terminal air companies in ignorance of the effect of such subsidy upon railroad passenger service and bus operations. Perhaps the silliest of our Federal air subsidies is that to the New York Airways, which provides helicopter service between the airports and midtown New York. Here the Federal Government pays more than $2 of subsidy for every dollar of revenue taken in from the public.

Without a Department of Transportation, pressure groups of one form or another are unrestrained. Indeed, each pressure group has its bureaucratic spearhead, and there is no point in the government today at which these pressures can be balanced against one another in terms of public interest. The result is that an important part of the Federal budget goes for transportation, and yet under today's lack of coordination, cooperation, and integration, no one is responsible for seeing that the best in each form of transportation is being encouraged, that excesses are being curbed, and that planning for the future is in competent and productive hands. A Department of Transportation would not, as some fear, put government further into transportation. It would introduce coherence, restraint, and responsibility into the present chaotic interference.

Other Proposals

There are a number of other practical steps that could relieve some of the crushing load imposed upon railroads by unsound public policy:

Featherbedding. On top of the featherbedding provisions in the railroads' contracts with unions lies a heavy weight of featherbedding by law. Many states have laws requiring excess crews. There are many "make-work" provisions under the guise of safety. Featherbedding represents waste for which the American people pay. It represents a great economic millstone upon the opportunity of the railroad industry to compete. The typical railroad worker is not an exponent of featherbedding, and I am sure that most railroad people would unhesitatingly prefer an equal opportunity to compete for the commerce of the country. [See "Featherbedding and Make-Work," and "It's Not Featherbedding," in Section III, below.]

Diversification. Railroads are not lawfully permitted, as a generalization, to engage in other forms of transportation. In this age of diversification, with opportunity for monopoly long since gone, what could be more reasonable than to permit any transportation enterprise to compete, if it desired, in the whole field of transportation? [See "Freight Wars and Freight Rates," in Section III, below.]

Taxation. The railroads, as large property owners in most states, have been and are seriously abused taxpayers. The confiscatory tax picture in New Jersey is well known. Railroad taxation there is higher than in any other state of the Union, so much so that few railroads operating in New Jersey have had any net income from New Jersey traffic during the postwar years.

Taxation in relation to earnings and impartially assessed against all forms of transportation would be a substantial forward step. [See "Taxing the Railroads out of Business," in this section, below.]

Consolidation.   An important development in the East is the proposed merger of the Erie and Lackawanna railroads into a combined system, which is now before the Interstate Commerce Commission awaiting approval.   Improved income of more than $13 million a year is anticipated from this unification, reflecting more intensive use of facilities and manpower. There must be more such mergers to produce improved service and improved utilization of equipment, track, and facilities. And the more quickly they occur in the East, the healthier this segment of the railroad industry will become.   [See "Four Systems for the Future," in Section III, below.]. . .

Because transportation is so vital to our industrial and social progress, the correction of the evils in transportation that I have described, and the restoration of opportunity for management to succeed or fail under equal ground rules, is one of the great contributions that we, as a people, can give our children.

Perhaps it would collaterally encourage an even greater contribution, namely, one toward reestablishing individual responsibility, toward lessening dependence of business enterprise upon government, and toward a philosophy of minimum governmental interference with business and individuals.

THE COMMUTER—PROBLEM ON WHEELS [3]

Out of a U.S. working force of 66 million, commuters make up a scant 10 million.   Yet their daily cycle from home to work accounts for a larger volume of passenger traffic than any other type of weekday travel.   Six million of them get to work and back home by auto, 450,000 by train, 3,500,000 by bus, subway or rapid transit.   Others ingeniously make the trip by airplane, helicopter, bicycle, motor scooter, powerboat and, in the case of one hardy California commuter, by kayak.

[3] From "Those Rush-Hour Blues," cover story. *Time.* 75:74-8. Ja. 18, '60. Courtesy *Time;* copyright Time Inc. 1960.

The great postwar exodus to Suburbia has scattered commuters through the U.S. countryside surrounding great cities, put a crippling strain on the arteries that feed the metropolises. A few foreign cities also have problems in handling the commuter torrent: London and Paris groan beneath its weight, Tokyo hires students to push commuters tightly into rush-hour trains, and Calcutta's commuter rails are so crowded that people ride prone on the roofs of coaches. But in the U.S., the nation-wide flight to the suburbs has created a huge problem for almost every major city. And the problem is due to get worse.

If vast transportation changes are not made, traffic experts predict that by 1970 so many cars will be pouring daily into big cities that the monstrous traffic jam will just about stop all movement. For U.S. commuter railroads, crying out in financial agony, the auto has wiped out much of the balanced, all-day, regular-fare business that once made rail passengers profitable. It has left the rails burdened with the money-losing, morning-evening commuter rush—and even cut heavily into that. The number of passengers commuting by rail annually has dropped from 458 million in 1929 to 224 million in 1959. . . . The commuter is thus a U.S. problem child—but he is also a precocious darling. He is vital to the business life of the big cities, as a group holds more responsible, higher-salaried jobs than his noncommuting brethren. Commuters earn more than $2 billion in New York City, $1.7 billion in San Francisco. The commuter is well-educated, aggressive, articulate—and, as a class, furiously united against everything that threatens to interrupt his daily nest-to-work cycle. . . .

The problems that the commuter poses to the nation's cities are great and prickly—but they are not unique. In the second century, the satirist Juvenal graphically described the swarming streets of ancient Rome. They were thick with litter bearers, chariot jams, and furious drivers who knocked people down and ran over them in their haste to get home to dinner. . . . But it was not until late nineteenth century London that the commuter appeared as a distinct type. London's rapid growth called for so much space for businesses that citizens were forced out of the center of the metropolis, had to commute to work by horse bus and rail. It was only in the United States, with its spreading cities and changing population patterns, that the commuter came into his own as a widespread social phenomenon. He got a big boost from the introduction of the cut-fare commutation ticket for those who ride the rails daily.

Just what sort of creature is the modern-day commuter? If he travels by rail, he is a man (few women are commuters) of almost inflexible habits. A slave to the timetable, he is often up before the farmers, and into bed before his teen-age sons. A single glance at his schedule can make him break off the most scintillating conversation in the city, or leave his wife in the midst of an embrace. He likes to dash for the train with seconds to spare, board it daily at the same precise spot on the platform, sit in the same seat. "You ought to hear the howls we get," says a New Haven trainman, "when the engineer brings the train in a few feet off the usual stopping place."

The commuter does not like to talk with strangers (or often with anyone), or wear double-breasted suits, or sit with a woman, or travel without a hat. To preserve his privacy, he uses his newspaper like a shield, or he plays cards with the same partners. If he reads a sexy book or a left-wing newspaper, it is prudently concealed between more respectable pages. Whether he reads or works on the train (some commuters carry pocket-sized gadgets for dictating), drinks in the bar car, or gazes idly at the countryside, he is likely to do the same thing every day. One Chicago commuter, accustomed to finding his grey Volkswagen in the same spot at the station every evening, hopped off the 6:28 one day, slipped behind the wheel of the car. He gave a cursory nod to the kids in the rear, leaned over to kiss his wife—and discovered to his horror that both she and the kids were total strangers. Retreating hastily, he hid behind a telephone pole until his wife showed up.

Some commuters insist that they undergo the daily trip to the big city and back for the sake of the wife and kiddies. There also are Freudian explanations. Says New York psychiatrist Dr. José Barchilon, himself a commuter:

The twice-daily sacrifice of the commuter to the indignities of transportation satisfies something deep within the husband's psyche. In modern society there are few opportunities for the breadwinner to endure personal hardship in earning the family living, such as clearing the forest or shooting a bear. For some husbands who spend their day in plush offices, the discomforts of commuting help alleviate feelings of guilt or envy that their wives are closer to primary hardships, *e.g.*, cooking, minding the children.

Many rail commuters welcome the trip as an hour of respite between frustrating tensions at the office and petty annoyances at home. Says a Stony Brook, Long Island-Manhattan commuter: "I commute to get a little peace and quiet each day. I have five kids."

But There Is No Peace

The man who drives his auto to work, on the other hand, can rarely relax. He prizes the independence the auto gives him, but he pays for it dearly. With one foot on the brake and the other on the accelerator, he braves traffic jams so packed that, so the story goes, a Los Angeles driver was carried along for ten miles after he ran out of gas. He can expect no quarter from his own. A motorist lost on the Santa Ana freeway recently pulled his car onto the center island to take his bearings. Three hours later he was still there, trapped by a whizzing flow of motorists who refused to slow down enough to let him get back on the road.

The total of U.S. cars is now 62 million, and it is growing faster than the population. Billions of dollars are being spent to build new roads and expressways that sometimes cost up to $30 million a mile. Los Angeles has spent $800 million in the last decade, Detroit $76.8 million since 1955, and Boston $125 million for a three mile central artery. For every acre of floor space constructed, suburban plants now need two acres of space for their commuting workers' cars. Some cities, notably Los Angeles and Detroit, devote up to two-thirds of their downtown areas to streets and parking areas.

Despite the auto's onward rush, the core of the commuter problem is still the railroads, the most efficient of the facilities for moving people in and out of big cities. A double-track commuter line can carry five times as many people per hour as a four-lane superhighway. To build enough highways for the 30,000 commuters who travel into Philadelphia on the Pennsylvania Railroad would cost $611 million. If everyone who now rides the trains into New York decided to drive, a third of Manhattan would be needed just for parking space. The auto is an inefficient commuter tool, carries only an average 1.7 commuters. Soviet Premier Khrushchev, inspecting crowded San Francisco highways, exclaimed what every American knows: "What a waste."

But if commuters need the railroads, most railroad men are sure that they can do without the commuter. Well over half of the 360 million people who ride trains each year are commuters, yet they contribute only 20 per cent of all passenger fares. Railroad men complain that for every $1 they get from the commuter, the road must spend up to $1.50 just to keep him moving. Many commuters are convinced that the bookkeeping is tricky, that the roads charge too big a share of passenger expenses to them. But the roads only conform to Interstate Commerce Commission bookkeeping regulations. The New Haven claims it lost $8.4 million on New York commuters last year. The New York Central lost $4.5 million on commuters, the Pennsylvania $10 million, the Southern Pacific $1 million, the Milwaukee $320,000. . . .

Fares and Taxes

One key to the railroads' financial plight is the commuter fare. Despite hefty hikes in the last few years, it is still one of the biggest bargains in the United States. For example, a commuter can ride on the New Haven between Manhattan and Larchmont, New York, a commuter bedroom nineteen miles from the city, for 50 cents a ride on a forty-six-ride commutation ticket—one fourth or less of what it would cost to drive his car, not counting parking fees. One reason for the low fares is that United States railroads still suffer from the bad reputation earned in the days of the Robber Barons, when as a monopoly, they often gouged the public. Now, though they are far from monopoly, they find it tough to get permission from the ICC and state utility commissions for fare increases. The Long Island Rail Road, biggest U.S. commuter line, was unable to get a fare hike from 1918 to 1947, despite repeated requests. Other railroads waited too long to press for hikes, let fares over the years fall far behind rising costs. Most claim that they now need 50 per cent to 70 per cent higher fares just to break even on the commuter.

"The commuter pays only a fraction of the cost," says the . . . [New York Central's assistant vice-president William R. Main] "and he doesn't see why he should pay more." But the commuter may soon have to change his thinking. The longer he resists fare hikes, the worse his lot may become. Any intelligent New Haven rider, for instance, knows that if the road cannot make money, it will go bust—and he will have to find another, more expensive way to work. Many roads fear that raising fares much more will drive more commuters to the auto. But the sturdy rail commuters still left have little taste for exchanging their lot for traffic chaos. The Long Island has raised fares four times since 1956, yet has never lost more than 1 per cent of its commuters after any hike.

Higher fares do not make the entire answer to the railroads' problems. The very nature of the commuter business—running at a peak for only four hours daily—means that roads must keep expensive equipment and labor idle for most of the day. "You couldn't profitably run a shoe factory or a bean cannery on such a schedule," says the Long Island's president, Thomas Goodfellow. "You can't profitably run a railroad that way either."

Railroads are also hobbled by books full of outdated and unnecessary regulations. . . . ICC Member Anthony F. Arpaia, who should know, [has] called the commission "an organizational monstrosity." Both the ICC and state commissions require months or years of hearings before railroads may drop obsolete runs. The New York Central struggled for five years to drop its West Shore line. It was losing $3 million annually —enough, said the Central's president, Alfred Perlman, "to have provided a Chevrolet, if not a Cadillac, for each of the less than four thousand commuters using the service." Railroad unions also add to costs by featherbedding, and full-crew laws in sixteen states force the roads to employ men they consider unnecessary, last year cost the Central $5 million in New York State alone.

For years the railroads have been hit for hefty taxes by every little town they pass through. They are also prime targets for states such as New Jersey, which, says the ICC, assesses rail property at 100 per cent of value while setting a lower base for other taxpayers. When a railroad repairs a bridge or improves a parking lot, it is not praised, but taxed more heavily. New York City forced the Central to build a new $23 million bridge over the Harlem River in such a way that a new highway could pass under it, then upped taxes on the bridge from $70,000 to $500,000 a year. Says the Central's solicitor, Robert D. Brooks: "Everyone wants to milk the cow, but no one wants to feed it."

The New Haven's [president George] Alpert thinks the solution to such problems is an all-out campaign for government subsidies. He charges that the railroads are slowly being crushed by subsidized competiiton. Says he:

> Subsidy is a common practice today, particularly in the field of transportation. Billions have been spent in the construction of airports for the use of the airlines. This is a subsidy. Hundreds of millions have been spent to maintain the merchant fleet, privately owned. This is a subsidy. For the benefit of the automobile and truck user, $93 billion has been spent on the highways, of which only $45 billion has come back in user charges. The balance is subsidy.

Alpert is particularly galled that the Government gave more than $2 million in 1958 subsidies to New York Airways' helicopter service, which carried fewer passengers all year (91,000) than the New Haven carries in a day. The Government has given loans and grants of more than $1 billion to aid foreign railroads, including one chunk for improving commuter service in Colombo, Ceylon. Says Alpert: "There would seem to be very little reason why some slight recognition should not be given by our Government to the railroads that are struggling for survival here in the United States."

Most of Alpert's fellow railroad men look on his plea for subsidy with the same disapproval they show of kids who throw rocks at trains. What they do want is equal treatment with all other forms of transportation, including tax equality or outright tax relief. In this, they have a shining example to encourage them: the Long Island Rail Road, which once vied with the New Haven in the race to ruin, now enjoys a reputation as the best New York commuter railroad.

What happened on the Long Island? Losses ran so high that its owner, the Pennsylvania Railroad, had the road thrown into bankruptcy. Even that brought no outside help. Not until two accidents in a year (1950) killed 109 commuters did New York State decree a twelve-year, $65 million rebuilding program. To give the road money for new equipment and better service, it excused it from all state taxes, many local taxes, allowed it to raise fares at will. [Since the Long Island Rail Road operates wholly within New York state it did not need the permission of the Interstate Commerce Commission to raise its fares; permission of the state's Public Service Commission was sufficient. For roads engaged in interstate commerce, even though the affected commuter lines are intrastate, ICC permission must be sought.—Ed.] The Pennsy agreed to give up for twelve years payments due it on $62 million in Long Island indebtedness. The plan halved the Long Island's tax bill, saves the road $2.3 million a year. President Goodfellow points out that the sum "is almost, but not quite, enough to build one mile of a six-lane expressway on Long Island." Encouraged by such success, New York State is trying partial tax forgiveness for other roads, to the tune of $1.5 million a year.

Even given higher fares and tax relief most U.S. railroads have yet to learn one basic lesson. It is that the transportation industry, in the words of Keneth M. Hoover, chief engineer of the San Francisco's Bay Area Rapid Transit District, "is in the business of selling rides, just as the corn flake business is in the business of selling corn flakes." One man who has learned this lesson well is Ben Heineman, the lawyer turned railroader who is chairman of the Chicago and North Western Railway. Heineman took over a $2 million- to $3 million-a-year money loser in 1956. For the commuter, fares went up, but Heineman gave him better service, more modern equipment. Last year the North Western made about $40,000 profit on commuters, has the healthiest and most promising commuter operation in the United States. . . . [Early in 1960] Heineman announced another step forward: the road will borrow $21 million to replace all the road's remaining obsolete equipment with the most modern equipment available. Says he:

> We refused to believe that the North Western, with the exercise of imagination, couldn't lick this commuting problem. It is our obligation to perform this social function, but just staying in it wasn't enough. We have broken a vicious circle by breaking with tradition.

But not even Ben Heineman has been spared the commuter's fondness for taking out all his ills—from a bad breakfast to a grouchy boss—on the railroads. Three months ago, commuters waiting at the North Western's Fort Sheridan station were speechless when a brand-new commuter train pulled in. Like urchins examining a Cadillac, they climbed aboard, bounced on the soft seats, gazed in wonder at the fluorescent lighting. Then the train started, and they noticed that the new type of brake, while safer, had an unfamiliar squeak. Muttered one: "You'd think that they'd have brakes that didn't squeak on equipment as expensive as this." Said another, "Yeah—is that what our last fare increase went for? It's a helluva way to run a railroad."

Some roads have actually found that the heart of the commuter can be touched. Chicago's Burlington railroad, rich from freight, modernized its passenger trains in 1948, then asked for a fare hike. Commuters were so pleased by the improvements that they even wrote letters to the Illinois Commerce Commission backing the request. Four more increases also went through smoothly. The Burlington hopes to slip into the black on commuters this year. Even if it fails, it feels that its commuter losses add up to a modest price to pay for the public's good will. Says the Burlington's president, Harry Murphy: "We've got to serve the commuters, so I believe we should give them the best service we can possibly afford."

The Philadelphia Story

Because they must serve the commuter—like it or not—other railroads and transit systems, along with cities, are also trying to find ways to do the job right. The Pennsylvania and Reading railroads and the city of Philadelphia are cooperating in "Operation Northwest," in which the railroads have stepped up service and lowered fares, and issue transfers for the city's transit system in return for a $320,000 grant to help cover extra costs. The plan has not cut commuter losses, but it has proved that the commuter can be won away from the auto: the Pennsy's passenger load has jumped 17 per cent, the Reading's 29.5 per cent. Operation Northwest, an experiment, served the fashionable Chestnut Hill area of Philadelphia. A similar plan called Operation Northeast, serving the more modest Fox Chase section, increased the passenger load by 200 per cent. Both experimental operations were so successful that in January 1960 the city, in cooperation with the two railroads and railroad labor, organized a nonprofit agency called the Passenger Service Improvement Corporation to carry them a step farther. Operating under a city subsidy in excess of $2 million the corporation will provide fast, frequent service from outlying parts of the city to midtown at 30 cents a ride, a reduction from the normal fare. The Pennsylvania and the Reading, acting as contract carriers for the corporation, are guaranteed fixed amounts. If the fares collected do not meet these guarantees a city subsidy will make up the difference.—Ed.]

San Francisco has formed the Bay Area Rapid Transit District to set up a regional network of 70-mile-per-hour rapid-transit trains that, when completed in 1965, will get commuters from any one station to any other in less than an hour. What spurred it on was a voter outcry against the blight on the city's beauty caused by superhighways. The state legislature decided that the motorist must help pay for the new system, will nick him for $115 million in traffic tolls to construct a rapid-transit tube under San Francisco Bay.

Atlanta Transit System switched from corner-to-corner bus lines to fast, limited runs, last year netted $87,197 in profits. Los Angeles Metropolitan Transit Authority went after business by labeling buses formerly marked "P" and "M" with such snappy names as "The Freeway Flyer" and "The Zephyr." They carry signs for the benefit of frazzled motorists: "Quiet, please. Our passengers are resting." Says a company official: "Same bus. You just snap a little life into the system and people will buy."

The penalty for failing to snap life into the nation's public transportation is to see many U.S. cities share the fate of Los Angeles. The rail commuter system that once operated 6,200 electric trains daily over 1,061 miles of track was a hit-and-run victim of cars. Since then, at a cost of $1.6 billion, the city has built 271 miles of freeways and 266 miles of expressways to accommodate some 2 million motorists—and is furiously working on 107 more. But, says Edward T. Telford, engineer in charge of construction, "it will be years before we can catch up to the need—if we ever can."

Taken as a composite, the Los Angeles commuter reels off some 39,330,000 miles a day just going to and from his job, the equivalent of 165 trips to the moon and back. Each day he generates 5.6 billion cubic feet of auto smog that has created a new problem for the city. If a car stalls for two minutes on a Los Angeles freeway, at least thirty minutes is needed to untangle the traffic jam. Says Sam Taylor, boss of the Los Angeles traffic department: "We talk casually about moving a man to the moon and back; yet we can't move the man to work and back so he can build the missile to take the man to the moon and back."

Behind the nation's commuter problem lies a woeful lack of public planning. Many new roads, good in themselves, have been built to dump autos on the city without providing tie-ins with transit systems that could ease downtown traffic congestion. By failing to coordinate Boston's new half-billion-dollar express-road system with the city's ailing Metropolitan Transit Authority, officials left no feeder roads where the M.T.A. could pick up passengers, helped accelerate the M.T.A. decline. Railroad lines and rapid-transit systems, which can often complement each other, frequently compete with each other—and the auto—because of lack of central planning.

> We're in trouble today [says San Francisco's Hoover] because for the last twenty years we have been putting our transportation eggs into one basket—the development of facilities for the private automobile to the virtual exclusion of every other form of transportation.

The answer to the problem, most experts agree, is neither to outlaw the automobile in cities, nor abandon the commuter to his fate. . . . What the nation's big cities need, if they are not to become monstrous masses of immovable autos, is better, more efficient public transportation. Traffic experts want to see the train, the bus and the rapid-transit system take their rightful place alongside the auto as part of a coordinated transportation system. In order to compete effectively, the railroads need tax equality and freedom from excessive regulation. The ICC has already come out in favor of tax relief, and Congress . . . [in 1958] made it easier for the rails to discontinue service that is no longer needed. Once these preliminaries are over, it is up to the railroads —and to the auto's other rivals—to win the commuter's hand by fervent wooing. The best suitor will win, but there are plenty of commuters to go around. Like all who feel underprivileged, put upon, unwanted and besieged, the U.S. commuter has a secret desire: he wants to be loved—and to get there on time.

THE 20-HOUR WEEK ON THE RAILROADS [4]

In March . . . [1958] the Public Service Commission finally granted the New York Central permission to discontinue its Putnam Division—a fifty-two-mile line running from New York City into Westchester County. A New York television station sent a camera crew and a commentator for a ride on one of the trains to get mass public reaction of riders to the discontinuance

[4] From article by David I. Mackie, formerly vice president and general counsel of the Delaware, Lackawanna & Western Railroad and now chairman of the Eastern Railroad Presidents Conference. *Reader's Digest*. 72:48-53. Je. '58. Copyright 1958 by The Reader's Digest Association, Inc. Reprinted with permission.

order. When the train pulled out, the TV crew found that there were only two passengers on the whole train—one in each car.

The incident reflects the devastating effects of the commuting business which are undermining the rail service of numberless communities from coast to coast.

To hundreds of thousands of commuters the railroads seem to have little cause for complaint. Every morning and evening they board coaches filled to capacity. They pay a steady monthly fee to the railroad and travel over tracks that, they are convinced, the railroads would have to use for through traffic even if there were no commuting business. What more could any industry want, they ask, than a steady, assured flow of capacity business to make full use of facilities that it has to keep in operation anyway? And so for years commuters have been waging a running battle with the rails to prevent them from raising fares or dropping trains from the schedule.

What are the facts?

Every weekday twenty-six of the nation's railroads haul about half a million people to their offices in the cities and back home again to the suburbs. New York's commuter load is the biggest— more than 200,000 round trips daily. In Chicago 150,000 people stream in every morning. The rest are clustered around San Francisco, Boston, Philadelphia, Pittsburgh, Washington and a dozen other cities. . . .

Take a look at the world's most concentrated commuter center, New York City. The daily ebb and flow of more than 200,000 commuters crossing the rivers surrounding Manhattan Island is one of the wonders of the railroading world. Railroad men come from scores of foreign countries to see it in operation. At the high points of the rush there is less than a minute between trains. So tight is the schedule that recently, when the New Haven (which shares Grand Central Terminal with the New York Central) tried to squeeze one more train into the peak-hour timetable, the schedules of more than thirty other trains had to be juggled to make room. Mechanically the picture is one of marvelous efficiency, but in every other respect it represents one of the worst messes in the railroad business.

The crux of the commuting problem lies in the "twenty-hour week." On each of the five weekdays, railroads must be prepared to handle four hours of peak traffic: a two-hour rush in the morning and a two-hour rush in the evening. But between these two peaks of travel is a deep valley. For the rest of the week-day, and practically all of Saturday and Sunday, the cars and crewmen needed to handle the commuter rush remain idle. These peaks and valleys constitute the basic reason why the railroads cannot avoid losing money on commuters.

First is the problem of equipment. The average New York commuter train can haul about twelve hundred people, and about three hundred such trains are needed to handle the city's rush-hour loads. These trains, using more than three thousand pas-senger coaches, represent an investment of hundreds of millions of dollars. But 83 per cent of the Jersey Central's commuter cars lie idle between peak and peak. For the Pennsylvania the figure is 90 per cent, and the figures for the other roads are com-parable. . . .

Tracks, yards, station facilities and highly complex signaling equipment are also essential to handle the commuters, and here again the railroads suffer from the peaks. Without commuters, even New York's Grand Central Terminal would be unneces-sary; the whole station could be moved from the high-priced heart of midtown to a point on the outskirts fully served by sub-ways and buses. With elimination of the terminal would also come elimination of the road's fantastically expensive tracks under Park Avenue.

Next comes the problem of labor. The two-peaked move-ment involves some labor costs straight out of Alice in Wonder-land. A ten-car commuter train in New York is by law required to carry a minimum crew of five men—engineer, fireman, con-ductor and two brakemen. Though the majority work only two trains a day, one inbound and one outbound, each man must be paid for a full eight-hour day once he has reported for work. If the timespread between his reporting for duty and signing out is more than nine hours, he is entitled to overtime for the excess. This sometimes results in startling pay scales. An extreme but by no means unique case is that of the engineer who makes one daily thirty-three-mile round trip between the suburbs and the city. He works about one hour and fifty minutes a day, or nine and a quarter hours a week. For this he makes (with overtime) $145.68, or $15.75 an hour. The railroads' labor costs per mile of commutation service run from two to three times the costs for long distance passenger trains.

The peak-hour mess also complicates the movement of freight and the jobs of the maintenance people. Schedules are frequently too tight and passenger trains move too fast to permit a stream of boxcars to mix into the traffic flow. This means that crack freight trains with valuable loads may have to wait for precious hours while the commuters rush by. The North Western, rather than even attempting to mingle freights with commuters, operates an entirely separate freight line northward from Chicago.

The rails are off-bounds to maintenance crews, too, during the rush. When trains are streaking by every few minutes, it is impossible for them to work. Safety requirements forbid it. Not only must commuting-line maintenance be squeezed into the non-peak hours, but the heavy traffic on these lines necessitates more maintenance than for less-traveled sections of track. It costs two to four times as much to keep a heavily used commuter right-of-way in shape as it does for the rest of the line.

While commuter service may mean only part-time use of valuable equipment, there is nothing part-time about the local property taxes levied on the railroads for the road-bed and stations that serve the commuters. Indeed, taxes hit the rails hardest in the commuter areas because these areas, being the most highly developed, have the highest tax rates.

The New York Central operates Grand Central Stattion largely for the benefit of commuters. But on the first five and a half miles of its track out of Grand Central the taxes are $6.2 million—more than 17 per cent of the total franchise and property taxes assessed against the entire 10,700-mile New York Central System. In other words, the highest taxes are paid on the stretch of road responsible for the Central's biggest losses.

All these higher costs would seem logically to justify higher per-mile fares for commuters than for long-haul passengers. But the fact is that commuters pay the lowest rate per mile of any railroad passengers.

This is due partly to the way the commutation service evolved. At the turn of the century when people began moving from the cities to the suburbs, the railroads wanted their patronage to fill up long-haul trains on the final leg of the journey. So the railroads offered them special rates, since the commuters could be absorbed in the normal traffic load. But as the Scarsdales, Winnetkas, Chestnut Hills and Palo Altos developed, extra trains had to be put on and the schedule began to sprout two lumps at either end of the day. The lumps gradually grew into peaks. Nobody knows exactly when the cost of supporting these peaks out-ran the income they provided, but it was probably in the twenties.

Ever since, the railroads have found themselves in a curious—and unique—position among publicly regulated utilities. Unlike gas and electric companies, which are allowed to charge a premium rate when the demand is heaviest, the railroads have to provide peak-demand service at a *discount*. In Chicago, the Milwaukee Railroad recently totted up the fifty-five fares it is allowed to charge between stations within the city where it competes with the Chicago subway system. Of the fifty-five fares, fifty-two were *below* the 25-cent subway toll.

For over a quarter of a century the railroads have been pleading for relief and during this period, as the commuting deficits have grown, the regulatory commissions have been parceling out too little, too late. The Long Island Rail Road, for instance, got a 10 per cent commutation rate rise in 1918 and spent the next twenty-nine years pleading for more. It finally got one in 1947, but it was too late; in 1949 it went bankrupt. The Long Island—almost exclusively a passenger line—had insufficient profits from freight to pay its commuter losses.

And as freight profits for all railroads continue to dwindle, most railroads with passenger service are finding themselves less and less able to write off passenger service costs against freight revenues.

Not only do the regulatory commissions make it extremely difficult for railroads to raise commuter rates; they sometimes make it next to impossible for them to eliminate even flagrantly unprofitable lines.

At hearings before state public service commissions commuters usually claim that the railroad's bookkeeping is "stacked" to show a commuter deficit, and that if the railroad would only provide better service and equipment it would attract enough new passengers to reduce losses. . . .

The fact is that the railroads cannot juggle their books. The Interstate Commerce Commmission enforces the strictest uniform accounting practices on the railroads. A non-profit research foundation recently made a study of the ICC's accounting methods and concluded that, if anything, the railroads are losing *more* money on passengers than their books indicate. . . .

As to cutting losses by improving service, the railroads have tried valiantly. In the last half-dozen years the New Haven and the New York Central have invested over $30 million in new air-conditioned coaches; the Boston & Maine has replaced several hundred turn-of-the-century coaches with the world's largest fleet of super-modern stainless-steel cars—108 of them at an average cost of $160,000 apiece. Since 1952 many other roads have engaged in similar modernization programs, and the national total for such improvements is well over $100 million. But the experience of all of them has been identical: few additional passengers were lured to the rails by the improvement in service.

The New York Public Service Commission recently put itself on record on the question of whether railroads can make money out of commuters. In a decision the commission—not noted for a soft-hearted attitude toward the railroad point of view—said: "Railroad passenger business, as presently conducted, is not and cannot be operated at a profit."

This raises the question: if the railroads cannot make a profit from passengers, and if their profit from freight is diminishing every year—what is to be done?

A perfectly logical solution is available. This is simply to apply to the communities which benefit from commuter service the principle applied to the customers of every public utility: "You must pay for what you get—or you can't have it." But no government agency has ever dared to lay down this law. The reason is that the commuting communities are many and vocal, and they naturally do not want to pay the full cost of the service. But the point is approaching where somebody other than the railroads will have to pay.

Two different situations must be dealt with. The first is where the public has abandoned the railroad commuter service to the degree that it is no longer essential to the functioning of a community—as in the recent case of the Putnam Division of the New York Central. In such instances the railroad must be allowed to abandon the service.

In the second situation—where the public demand for the commuting service is so great that the service obviously must be continued—the money-losing commuter operation no longer can be considered a private business. It is a public service and should be paid for by the public. Suggestions as to how the public, rather than the railroads, should foot this bill range from outright subsidization of the railroads to the lowering of local real-estate taxes or the raising of fares to a profitable level.

Regardless of the method, it is obvious that, as one railroad official has put it, "the railroads simply have to get this commuter monkey off their backs." Otherwise it may ride them straight into bankruptcy.

TAXING THE RAILROADS OUT OF BUSINESS [5]

On the edge of the Blackfeet Indian Reservation in Montana's Glacier County lies the town of Cut Bank (pop. 4500). Surprisingly, this small community boasts a large and expensive airport: it cost about $4 million of Federal funds and it covers three times the area of New York's La Guardia Airport. Only one carrier, Western Airlines, uses this field. In 1958 about two

[5] From "Must We Tax the Railroads out of Business?" article by David I. Mackie. *Reader's Digest*. 75:81-5. Ag. '59. Copyright 1959 by The Reader's Digest Association, Inc. Reprinted with permission.

passengers a day boarded its planes there. But the townspeople feel an airport is so important that they are willing to pay for its maintenance by keeping its 1,703 acres off the tax rolls and assessing a special annual airport tax against local property owners.

On the face of it, this makes sense. If the citizens are willing to pay for an airport, well and good. But when you examine who paid what in this case, the logic becomes a little blurred. In 1958 the Great Northern Railroad, which runs through Cut Bank and is therefore a local taxpayer, was assessed $2,530 as its share of the costs of this competing facility; in the same year Western Airlines paid $41.17.

But if you should accuse Cut Bank of unfairness to the Great Northern, the city fathers could point out that in whacking the railroad hard with local taxes they were only following well-established practice. Some of our biggest cities—New York, Cleveland, Boston, Pittsburgh, to name just a few—are masters of this art, and thousands of smaller taxing bodies are also practicing it with a will. In 1958 the bills of all these state and local tax collectors added up to a railroad tax of *$400 million* (in addition to $550 million in Federal income and payroll taxes). More than any other single factor, it is this huge sum that is causing our railroads frantic concern over what a 1958 Senate report called "the general decline of the railroads."

While the rails have seen their revenues increase less than 1 per cent a year over the past decade, their state and local taxes have climbed at the rate of more than 3 per cent annually. There are two reasons for the railroads' concern: the sheer size of the taxes, and the relationship between the railroads' taxes and those paid by their fast-growing competitors.

The first problem stems from the fact that the railroads are the largest industrial owners of real estate in the United States, with 386,000 miles of track taking them into 96 per cent of our 3,067 counties. This means that their rails run through literally thousands of individual tax jurisdictions—states, cities, towns, villages and school districts—to which every year they must contribute. In New York State alone the railroads contribute to more than 6,000 taxing bodies.

If these taxes had some logical relationship to the railroads' earnings in each community, the system might make some sense. But there is no such relationship.

In New Jersey, the Pennsylvania Railroad paid $5.8 million in taxes last year while earning only $700,000 [in the entire state].

In Toledo, Ohio, the local newspapers and the chamber of commerce conducted a campaign to force the New York Central to build a new passenger station, though the old station was already running at a deficit. The Central did build a new terminal, at a cost of $4,856,000, and the annual tax on it jumped from $8484 to $48,799.

In Pittsburgh, the Pennsylvania Railroad spent $9.5 million in realigning its tracks and rebuilding its passenger shed as part of the city's Golden Triangle redevelopment program—and immediately got slapped with a tax boost of $31,000 annually on the improvement.

And whenever the construction of a new highway or the improvement of an old one necessitates building an overpass or changing a grade crossing—which happens hundreds of times every year—the railroad not only has to contribute to the construction bill but finds itself paying more in taxes for the improvement.

Exorbitant overvaluation of railroad facilities for tax purposes is a temptation that many local politicians cannot resist. Jersey City, New Jersey, a major rail center with vast yards, is a case in point. When one railroad serving this city sold thirty-three acres recently—just to cut down on its crushing tax burden—the land, assessed at $621,296, sold for $19,472.

One of the odd results of the multiplicity and overlapping of tax jurisdictions is that the railroad industry contributes more tax money directly to education than does any other private institution. Every year about 60 per cent of the railroads' property taxes in Illinois go to education. In 1956, 45 per cent of the Pennsylvania Railroad's $32 million state and local taxes went to schools. In School District No. 7 of Lincoln County, Montana, the Great Northern pays 91.38 per cent of all school taxes levied in the district—despite the fact that the railroad's property comprises only one third of 1 per cent of the land. Altogether, the railroads' state and local tax bill for education in 1958— an estimated $140 million—was equal to almost a third of the Federal Government's contribution to the same school systems.

How the railroads' huge tax payments compare with those of their competitors is the other half of the picture. Here again the problem goes back to the fact that the railroads own so much real estate: stations in the hearts of cities, freight yards in their outskirts, and hundreds of thousands of miles of track from coast to coast. All this they build and maintain themselves, and on all of it they pay taxes.

But who builds, maintains and owns the airports, the waterways and the highways? By and large it is the government, and the government pays no tax. Nor, in any sense comparable to the railroads, do the airplanes, barges and trucks that use these facilities.

The airlines and water carriers pay nothing at all toward the construction and maintenance of their rights of way and signaling systems. The trucking industry does pay taxes in the form of registration and mileage fees, and in fuel and equipment levies. But these are merely *user* charges, intended to do no more than contribute toward highway construction, maintenance and administration costs. (In fact, the truckers insist that all Federal automotive excise taxes be earmarked exclusively for highway purposes.)

The railroads, on the other hand, without a cent of government subsidy, pay the *full* costs of building, maintaining and administering their rights of way, and it is the railroads, and the railroads alone, that must pay *additional* hundreds of millions of dollars toward the administrative costs of general government of the communities through which they run.

In New York City the railroads pay about $9 million in taxes on their passenger facilities. How much of this goes to support the city's two giant airports, La Guardia and Idlewild, it is impossible to estimate. Certainly some does, since these two fields pay no taxes.

Boston's 2,000-acre Logan International Airport, which cost $74 million of city, state and Federal funds, is not taxed at all. But the New Haven Railroad's thirty-one-acre South Station in downtown Boston pays the city over $1 million every year in taxes—about the same as the user fees paid by all the airlines using Logan.

In Illinois the railroads paid $32 million in property taxes in 1955. The 244 truck lines doing business in the state, the 17 certificated airlines and the 65 barge and towing companies paid $800,000.

The one encouraging glimmer of light for the railroads is the fact that more and more people are beginning to worry about this situation. Early this year a report to the governor of New York by his special assistant on transportation admitted that the state's treatment of the railroads was grossly unfair, and went on to say that this was actually costing the state money in the form of lost business and employment. As a result, the legislature has already enacted measures to alleviate the situation to some degree. In West Virginia railroad tax reform is likewise before the lawmakers.

At the Federal level, Senator George A. Smathers of Florida has conducted long and deep-probing hearings into the rail situation. The report of his subcommittee recommends that state and local governments reexamine railroad taxes to correct the "inequitable tax situation."

The problem is such a pressing one that the air is suddenly full of suggested solutions. Some observers suggest that railroad property used in connection with *passenger* service should be exempted from taxation, since it is easily demonstrable that the railroads lose money on passengers. Others favor some kind of government subsidy for the railroads, to offset the subsidies their competitors get. There are even some who think that the solution lies in slapping heavier taxes on the railroads' competitors.

All these suggestions ignore one basic fact. It is our national policy to treat our so-called "highways of commerce"—roads, airways, canals—as precious national assets and to keep them free of taxation. Why, then, should this policy not apply to the railroads? Certainly, in terms of the tonnage they carry, these are the most important transportation arteries of all. Why must they pay *any* property taxes?

Despite the apparent logic of such reasoning, nobody has yet dared to voice this suggestion. Property taxes are traditionally the province of the states, and who wants to stand up in public and ask the states to cut down the tree that rains $400 million into their treasuries every year?

But somebody will have to start talking in these stark terms soon. For this tax shakedown is inflicting such deep financial wounds that the railroads' very existence is threatened.

RAILROADS VERSUS THE COMMUTER [6]

The propaganda for subsidies necessitates an examination of the validity of the railroads' position. The railroads, let it be said at once, have a case. One of the strongest angles of this case is the tax situation. This is a legacy from the days when railroads were virtually the only means of travel and waxed so rich that they represented a veritable gold mine for local taxing authorities. Now they are hurting financially; but a tax, once imposed, is hardly ever reduced. [See the preceding article, "Taxing the Railroads out of Business."] The railroads contend—and almost every student of the problem agrees—that the onerous taxes imposed upon them are crushingly discriminatory. They point out that literally billions of dollars in public funds have been poured out on thruways, tunnels and bridges—facilities for which trucks and buses pay little more than token taxes, but which enable them to undercut the railroads. Airports and airlines are likewise the beneficiaries of whopping public subsidies. Only the railroads are compelled to pay their full way and to shoulder back-breaking taxes.

All of this is true, but government, like the railroads, is caught in a financial snarl. If New York and three suburban counties, for example, grant the New Haven a subsidy by cutting some $1.9 million off its tax bill, the money is going

[6] From an article by Fred J. Cook, journalist, magazine writer, and commuter. *The Nation.* 187:467-71. D. 20, '58. Reprinted by permission.

to have to come out of the pockets of the average taxpayer, whose back is already no less over-burdened with taxes than is the railroad's. Many rail executives themselves feel that it would be unfair to impose this burden on the over-taxed citizen who does not use the railroads, but they can see no other solution.

On the surface, then, it might seem that the railroads are entitled to subsidies and inevitably must get them; but judgment in such a complicated jungle as this should not be formed on surface indications. Primarily, the public and its official representatives should decide just how much of the railroads' anguished bleat is fact and how much is propaganda. Commuters protesting the unceasing fare increases have long contended that the railroads gimmick their accounting procedures, loading an unfair proportion of costs on passenger service as compared to freight.

The railroads' estimate of a $723.5 million loss on passenger service in 1957 is based on a formula approved by the ICC. This Federal regulatory agency, however, has long been suspected of being too closely in cahoots with the lines it is supposed to regulate, and recently it has even placed its official imprimatur on the railroads' own cries of doom. Many independent rail experts hold that a sounder formula than the ICC's would water down the staggering passenger loss to no more than $100 million; and some believe that the railroads actually continued to make money on passenger service until just a few years ago.

A specific example of the kind of financial hot air that occasionally balloons railroad statements of fantastic losses was furnished . . . when the New York Public Service Commission turned a spotlight on the New Haven. In December, 1957, [George] Alpert, the line's president, had said the road was losing $15 million annually on its passenger operations. On another occasion, the loss was put at $12 million. Still a third figure was given by Alpert in January 1958, testifying before a Senate subcommittee: he said the New Haven was losing $8 million annually on commuter service. Subsequently, New Haven official spokesmen corrected the figure to $7.7

million. Yet even the $7.7 million "loss" was arrived at only
by ignoring some impressive millions in income. For example,
the New Haven had collected $2.6 million from the sale of
186 pieces of property in 1957, but this little item was
omitted in arriving at the "loss" figure because it wouldn't be
"proper accounting procedure" to regard it as revenue [i.e., it
would be "non-recurring" income]. Under some prodding from
the PSC, it turned out that these millions had some equally
unacknowledged company. The New Haven admitted that it
had collected $2 million in rentals from four major New York
hotels and some apartment houses built on its property; but
this, said the railroad, was "non-operating" revenue and therefore it would be "obviously unfair" to consider it in calculating
profit and loss from passenger operations. The fact remains
that a "loss" figure that had started out at $15 million had been
steadily watered down until only $3.1 million was left. What
other less obvious items might be turned up in a minute
analysis of the New Haven's ledgers, no one knows; but it
would seem the public ought to know—and know definitely—
before it agrees to tax itself another $1.9 million annually for
the New Haven's benefit.

If one needs further proof of the necessity for extreme
caution in assessing railroad figures, one has only to consider
disclosures made . . . on a petition by the New York Central
Railroad to abandon its station at Philipse Manor, a growing
commuting area in rich Westchester County north of New
York. The railroad tried to show that the station was a financial
drag by listing, among other expenses, $3,710 for local real-estate
taxes; but at a public hearing it developed that this was a
bloated figure. Taxes on the station itself were just $900; the
$3,710 figure was arrived at by adding taxes on 9.32 acres of
choice real estate belonging to the railroad.

Even more embarrassing for the Central was the way its
carefully-compiled figure on Philipse Manor commuter travel
boomeranged. In a day-by-day compilation, the Central attempted to prove that one train was boarded by just thirty persons, another by twenty, another by a mere four. Unfortunately

for the railroad, the day for which the traffic was listed was May 30, Decoration Day, a holiday when the trains that the Central had said carried this little handful of commuters weren't running. The same tactical error was repeated by the Central when it listed traffic for July 4. This double blooper suggested to some unkind souls that the entire schedule had been faked; but the Central angrily said not so, some minor stupid clerk had just become confused copying off the figures.

In any event, the crudity of some of these financial distortions seems reminiscent of the days when railroads bought up entire state legislatures and rode roughshod over public opinion. Obviously, some basic changes are needed in this attitude before the railroads are permitted to tap the public till for subsidies.

What is basically needed is a full, Kefauver-type investigation to peel away the layers of phoniness from the railroad financial maze and to get at some basic truths. Even beyond this, railroad executives must be willing to make some radical changes in their thinking before heavy subsidies could conceivably be justified.

Granting the tax situation is inequitable, granting that commuter service is a drain because the roads must pay idle train crews for the lay-over time that separates night and morning rush-hours, the basic flaw in the railroad picture is the frozen mentality of most railroad executives. Rail passenger service simply cannot continue to exist if the railroads insist on committing suicide by raising fares to the point where they are no longer competitive with buses and airlines.

As Robert E. Bedingfield pointed out in the New York Times, "The business of the Pennsylvania and the Central has shrunk each time fares have been raised." And the Journal of Commerce, expressing the view that further hikes in commuter fares might be necessary, acknowledged the danger that this might only make a bad situation worse. "With each fare increase, traffic by rail dwindles and more spills out onto the highways," the Journal conceded sadly.

It seems obvious that what is needed, before subsidies, before anything else, is some daring and imagination on the part of railroad executives. There are some encouraging signs that an approach designed to make rail service faster, cheaper, more competitive, may woo back lost business and even in time restore profits.

The Missouri Pacific . . . [in 1958] slashed fares, offered cut-rate sleeping accommodations, improved service and served low-cost meals to coach passengers on its streamliner, the Colorado Eagle. The *Wall Street Journal,* reporting on this experiment . . . noted: "Mopac is pulling passengers from competing railroads, buses and even airlines in this mid-America area." With reference to the railroad's reduction of round-trip coach fare, first-class fare and Pullman charges on its Houston-to-Brownsville run in May, the *Journal* said: "In the first month passenger revenues jumped around 20 per cent above a year earlier. And the gains are continuing."

A similar experiment is now being attempted on commuter lines serving Philadelphia—so far with a similar result. Philadelphia appropriated . . . [funds] on the promise of the Pennsylvania and the Reading to step up commuter and off-hour service to the northern residential suburbs. The Philadelphia city fathers explained that they did not regard the . . . [appropriations] as an actual subsidy, but merely as an underwriting of increased operational costs to see if improved rail service would take some of the clutter of cars off city highways. If this could be done, the pressure for ever larger highways, ever more bridges and tunnels, ever increasing parking facilities would be eased, and a subsidy to the railroads, even from the taxpayers' standpoint, would justify itself.

The New York *Herald Tribune* reported . . . [in November 1958] on the Philadelphia experiment at the end of the first month of a six-month test period. The Pennsylvania had increased the number of trains on its Chestnut Hill run by 33 per cent to thirty-six daily; service was stepped up to every fifteen minutes in rush hours, every half-hour in off-hours. The Reading boosted the number of its trains from thirty-three to thirty-six daily, Saturday service on both lines was almost doubled, and cheaper fares were tied in with bus-line transfers. The result: In the fourth week of operation, the Pennsylvania carried 4,133 more passengers than it had in the test week of October 6, before the plan went into effect, a gain of 14.8 per cent; and the Reading picked up 2,422 passengers in the same week, an improvement of 7.6 per cent over its test week in May. For the entire four weeks, the Pennsylvania gained 11,128 additional riders; the Reading 7,099. The effect on city traffic already was observable; 600 fewer automobiles a day were coming into the city from the suburbs.

Philadelphia hopefully assessed the advantages of the plan this way: Cheaper fares mean a saving, for the individual commuter, of 90 cents a day over automobile operation (including parking fees, insurance and fuel costs), or a total of $100 in the six months of the test period. This saving to the individual driver is projected into a much greater saving to the city. It means, Philadelphia estimates, that about $1 million annually can be saved on the cost of maintaining existing roads and providing police protection. And this is apart from the merry-go-round cost of building ever more and wider highways.

The Mopac and Philadelphia plans, if they continue to grow and fulfill their promise [for an extension of the Philadelphia plan see "The Commuter: Problem on Wheels," in this section, above] offer this hopeful ray of light in an otherwise grim picture: the railroads could recoup their losses, regain lost business; they could receive the tax relief to which they are entitled (and this could be given without cost, perhaps even at an ultimate saving, to the taxpayer); and lastly, the commuter and the shopper could be given some of the twentieth-century creature comforts and service to which they are entitled.

But all of this can happen only if railroad management exhibits the kind of vision that will bring rail travel in line with the realities of the twentieth century. Subsidies are not justified and should not be given merely to allow a bad situation to continue to deteriorate. Even with subsidies, a continuation of present trends on most lines would mean steadily dwindling traffic, steadily declining revenues and the ultimate inevitability of government operation. If this should happen, the railroads should not be permitted to shuck off on government the unprofitable passenger business that they have helped to run into the ground while retaining the freight haulage on which they may still make a profit. For the public's welfare, if government operations has to come, it should embrace both passengers and freight.

Since the railroads obviously do not wish to be put completely out of business, they should be induced to accept the alternative of sensible, forward-looking cooperation. Let's find out what is the real truth behind the maze of propaganda figures that paint a horrible specter of colossal railroad losses. Let's find out what the railroads intend to offer in the way of more modern and complete service before we embark on a round of ever-increasing subsidies. And let's make sure that the railroads do offer what they should offer—the kind of service that will lure back the riders they should logically have and that will reduce the ever-mounting expenses of superhighways, traffic policing and parking. Only such a policy can insure the continued existence of the railroads as a private enterprise, operated with benefit to all.

TRAINS AND THE MIND OF MAN [7]

What makes me sad in these days of the decline of railroads is that I see in it the decline of an art as well as of a business. I do not suppose that when the public hears of another train or line being abolished, many people think of the railroad as a model of human thought. They grumble at the loss of a convenience around which they had shaped their habits. But the truth remains that the railroad was the first great embodiment of modern organization—that prophetic coordination of space, time, matter and men which we now consider the most natural thing in the world. We take it for granted that life will run on schedule;

[7] From article by Jacques Barzun, provost and dean of faculties of Columbia University and author of *The House of Intellect* and *God's Country and Mine. Holiday.* 27:11-22. F. '60. Reprinted by permission.

we are sure there is a timetable for everything, a name and number for every object, a supreme regularity and uniformity on which we can rely for the easy pursuit of our urgent purpose and imperious desire. We go to the proper place, ask "information," and buy our ticket. Nothing is more simple, regular, universal. Indeed, when Dostoevski wanted to express one of his characters' revolt against the universe (in *The Brothers Karamazov*), he made the man say that he "wanted to give back his ticket."

Dostoevski's image was new and striking but it inverts the chronological sequence. The railroad, in its precision and scope, imitated the universe of rotating spheres that run on schedule to the minute, each on its own track, as Aristotle knew, and from which he drew a model for all existence. But in Aristotle we have only a theory, literally a vision. For mankind actually to achieve the same complex perfection and make it work required a revolution in manners and in thought.

Cast your mind back to the first railroads and visualize that new creature, the signalman, once a farmer, now sitting in a box on a hilltop, pulling levers, ringing bells, writing numbers in a big book, and doing this for twelve hours on end—all to make a few hundred people or tons of coal, moving at speed, pass by a similar load along a stretch of track as isolated as the man and his box. Think of this, and you realize what imagination and social discipline were needed before heedless humanity could look upon the occupation as normal, as a career full of dignity and moral significance.

Older societies understood coordination of effort in war; they had religious ceremonies and administered laws according to plan; and they trained troupes of performers to act and sing in concert. There were order, imagination and beauty in all these activities. But the purpose was immediate and concentrated in time and space; the performers knew and were close to one another.

Compared with this, the scattered army of railroad men obeying codes and signals is what an abstract design of lines and angles is to the palpable likeness of a cow—indeed, it is as dot-and-dash compared to the spoken word.

The timetable, that bit of common paper bearing little more than numbers and algebraic signs, is an epitome of the new mode of life ushered in by the railroad. The timetable not only sums up the power to combine and predict from a distance the daily movements of those little worlds called trains but it also typifies the compulsion exerted by numbers and clocks and colored lights over the will of the natural rebel, man.

Before trains, travelers and their carriers were rival potentates bent on proving each his own superiority. As the customer paying his way, flaunting his title or his wealth, the traveler took as long as he liked to dine at the inn. As the holder of the reins controlling the motive power, the coachman played the despot about stopping and leaving. The handful of passengers formed an unruly colony split into cliques. We find their quarrels delightful in the picaresque novel down to *Pickwick*, and we bemoan the passing of a truly individualistic age, but its actuality would strike us as the anarchism of braggarts and delinquents. Our habitual self-discipline in public, our sense of social equality, our considerateness for others, are the manners of the age of trains, which is to say, the moral philosophy of the timetable.

From this philosophy it followed also that the natural rhythms of man's life, measured by sun and season, yielded to the ceaseless, intemperate urgency of multitudinous desires. In the stupendous working of a railroad the stretch of effort is continuous—there is no night or day, but the eternal rolling of the planet, alive with blinking lights and scarred with rails over which tons of matter traverse space with superhuman speed. And because this dynamic edifice can momently break up in disaster, only war approaches it in dramatic effect.

To gauge how new, how singular a departure from ancestral habit the railroad required, one has only to read its early history. The very power that we now instinctively respect was difficult to grasp: at the inauguration of the Liverpool and Manchester Railway in 1830, William Huskisson, member of Parliament and former president of the Board of Trade, was killed by an engine shunting among the crowd. No one knew how to gauge speed and distance, how and where to move; man's reflexes were inadequate to protect him in the midst of machines many times stronger than the horse and the ox, and as devoid of friendliness as of sense perception. Never to be domesticated, the machine would force man to superdomesticate himself.

But even a decade after the Liverpool disaster, the insouciance of natural man is still visible in dozens of historic facts. When one of the great pioneers of locomotive and bridge design, Brunel, wanted to know what happened to one of his engines, overdue at the terminal, he would mount another and drive her along the expected track of the missing train. Someone asked him what he would do if he rounded a corner and came face to face with the prodigal. No one knows how serious he was when he replied, "I would put on all the steam I could command, with a view to driving off the opposite engine by the superior velocity of my own."

The new disciplining of man's mind was difficult. It called for a grasp of the whole which was given to few—notably the government engineers charged with investigating accidents. Company directors resented the investigators' "minute and irresponsible interference"; they resistd "newfangled" mechanical improvements not only on the grounds of expense but also from deep-rooted resistance to forethought. Engine drivers were as mulish: when their boilers were first supplied with safety valves, they would screw these down tight, preferring to blow up rather than to lose steam. In the old code of brainless courage and improvised intelligence, taking precautions seemed unmanly, ignoble.

Standardization and system were similarly resisted. When in 1840, Thomas Edmondson, a Quaker who had failed in business and was employed as "booking clerk," proposed the use of printed and numbered tickets, the directors of the Newcastle and Carlisle would have nothing to do with it. The true, freeborn, Englishman's way to board a train was to have a sheet of particulars written out afresh each time, a sort of bill of lading for each passenger, with his name on it misspelled in full. When Edmondson's idea was tried, it was over a short stretch of a competing line.

So strong was the faith in free will absolute that it took police force and some horribly predestined accidents to keep people from riding on top of the coaches on excursion days. In France, to prevent impulsive exits from moving trains, the passengers were locked in before departure, a paternal solicitude which led to a fearful holocaust on the Versailles line in May 1842. If we add these object lessons to those learned by company directors from damage suits following accidents, we can appreciate the sardonic observation Charles Francis Adams made after the Civil War, that, unlike battle casualties, those resulting from railroad accidents have served humanity by forcing improvements. Usually, the mechanical device was ready; the obstacle, always, was the mind. The victory was to force people to think, and to act on the results of their thoughts.

Finally, after seventy-five years, The Railroad as idea and fact reached the fullness of its being. By the turn of the century it was an institution, an image of man, a tradition, a code of honor, a source of poetry, a nursery of boyhood desires, the sublimest of toys and the most solemn machine—next to the funeral hearse —that marks the epochs in man's life. Compared to a train, a vessel leaving or arriving lacks emotional weight and urgency. It has to sink before we are touched. But a train steaming in at night, in the rain, panting briefly and departing with impatient tolling or insistent shrieks while colored lights change or dwindle among those that stay—that is an emotion which cannot be taught or blunted by use.

The railroad imposed its language—sidetrack, shunt, derail, highball, let off steam—and also its architecture. The tunnels and terminals, the huge glass-and-metal sheds, the trestles and bridges are the great works of the last century and the forerunners of today's distinctive "skeleton" architecture. The railroad brought the world from wood and stone to iron and steel. Without coal in quantities that only a train could haul, no industry could exist.

It is hard to conceive that so great a transformation could have happened between Stephenson's teakettle of the 1820's and the Great Exhibition of 1851. This is what gives substance to my fancy of the railroad as agent and symbol of a mental revolution. Here lies the difference between the social organization of an ant heap and the social organization which men may be slowly evolving from its first large-scale model, the railroad. Destroy an ant heap and the creatures are so single-minded that they remake it exactly as before. But between the first great lines laid down in Britain and America 120 years ago and the modern national and transcontinental systems, there is not merely a technological and practical but a philosophical difference. Not only railroads have changed, but populations—and this largely through the intellectual influence of the railroads. Within a century mankind has—I will not say learned—but begun to understand that by giving up some trivial satisfactions of the self, it can gain realms of unsuspected freedom. System—the printed and numbered ticket—gives the freedom of movement which is potentially the indefinite extension of time. If my ego suffers from not seeing my name on the ticket, if I have to "personalize" my every act, I can always send myself a wire.

Why then the gloom about the railroads? They have done their part in educating and mobilizing mankind. Is it not inevitable that they should be displaced by faster and better means of transport? Faster, yes, but better is still to be proved. For in the displacement, it is clear the railroad's special virtue is being lost and not merely transferred. Nowhere in other forms of locomotion does the observant citizen find in front of him the vivid and awe-inspiring lesson of order and rationality embodied. Certainly not in the blithe anarchy of air and bus travel. The private car, which goes from door to door, compels work at the increasingly mindless task of driving while preventing any more agreeable use of time. Who has ever read a good book on the New Jersey Turnpike or enjoyed gin rummy while driving across the alkali desert? As for brute efficiency, the railroad is still supreme: five men running a fast freight will haul at less cost a tonnage which it takes two hundred trucks and drivers to transport.

But, I repeat, it is not efficiency or safety or comfort that concerns me. Rather, I grieve to see the most advanced physical and social organization of the last century go down in shabby disgrace for lack of the same comprehensive imagination that built it up. The decline is shabby in spite of practical advance. Diesel-electric engines; noiseless, dustless coaches, made to sit and think in; centralized and even automatic train control are triumphs of the technological mind. It is the other kind of mind that is wanting, beginning with the will of the companies to survive and to satisfy the public by inventiveness and skill. As the late Robert Young spent himself in pointing out, as president and critic of several roads, intellect has not for a good while been applied to the institution as a whole. It is still more often the hog and not the passenger that can travel from coast to coast without changing cars, and the excuse of management seems to be: "We discriminate only because equal treatment would mean expecting too much of the hog."

East of the Mississippi the quality and morale of train crews has gone down. The conductor, once the peer of the ship's captain, is now overworked, distrait and often rude. On the once great lines, accidents and breakdowns and delays are shamefully frequent, the result (one supposes) of inattention. The invasion of terminals and cars by vulgar advertising displays are so many signs of a cultural disintegration.

The lower ranks of train men make it clear that railroading no longer draws on the most intelligent and ambitious. Few Edisons, railroad presidents, or future authors are being molded to a discipline at the telegraph key or in the baggage car. And naturally, when the locomotive footplate turned into the upholstered seat of a Diesel, the delicate mastery of the ways of steam which fireman and driver had to possess was replaced by the simpler art of reading an ammeter and knowing how to decelerate by turning a handle. The difference is symbolic: the modern railroad train starts itself: all you have to do is stop it, as if it were coasting downhill.

Well, so be it. Repining will not change anything. But nothing that has ever been transcendent—as the railroad has been in the history of Western man—can ever itself be transcended. It remains a high point to which future generations will look back in wonder—"How did they do it?" But before they can ask the question, even under their breath, they will have to possess what we lack: almost as much genius as those who made the thing to wonder at.

III. THE ROAD AHEAD

EDITOR'S INTRODUCTION

To the official handicapper of a yacht race, anxious that each vessel have an equal chance of winning, the ideal race would be one in which all the entries finished in a dead heat for first place. To the Interstate Commerce Commission the ideal freight rate structure would be one in which any shipper in any part of the country could put his particular product in any market in the country at exactly the same transportation cost as any of his competitors. Neither ideal has ever been achieved, nor will be. A triple dead heat for first is the closest a handicapper has ever come; and the fact that California asparagus can reach the New York City market at approximately the same freight cost as Florida asparagus is more a groping towards the ideal than its complete realization. For New Jersey and New Mexico raise asparagus, too, as do North Carolina and North Dakota. And people in Chicago and Minneapolis buy it as well as people in New York.

When the problem created by a bunch of asparagus is multiplied by the scores of thousands of products that are produced and sold throughout the United States, then multiplied again and again to accommodate the additional factors imposed by the entry of trucks, barge lines, and pipelines into the national transportation complex, the enormousness of the task facing the ICC and the railroads that Gilbert Burck discusses in the second article of this section becomes apparent. And if freight rates were the only problem facing the railroads their future would appear much brighter, for quite possibly there is a mechanical brain on the drawing boards that will solve it at the push of a button.

Unfortunately, there are other problems. Some, such as commuters, taxes, government interference, and the inroads of the automobile, have been examined in the preceding section. Others, such as labor relations, the replacement and improving of equipment, the constant threat of war, are discussed in the articles that follow. All are tremendous problems, but they are not insoluble. The problems of labor will be solved, as they have been in the past, by the men who do the labor, the railroads that employ them, and the government and the laws that regulate both. The problems of maintenance and equipment will be solved by a combination of native intelligence and national legislation that will ensure continuation of the progress described by John A. Conway in the opening article. And the overriding problem—the problem of guaranteeing the United States an adequate, efficient, and stable railway system—will perhaps be solved by some amalgam of the suggestions advanced by the administration and by Mr. Burck in the article that concludes this book. The solution will not come tomorrow or next week or next month, but it will come.

THE RAILROADS FIGHT BACK: DIESELS, DOMES, AND DEBENTURES [1]

The storied railroad minstrel who sang of the mythical *Wabash Cannonball,* with its limitless schedule and "doozy" trappings, would find today that his dream train would barely qualify to haul second-string freight. Even much more recent dreams have faded at the spectacle of a railroad revolution that has revamped, revitalized, and just about rebuilt the vast U.S. railroad industry during the past ten years. . . .

The job was gigantic—the roads have spent almost $11 billion since V-J Day on equipment, tracks, and terminals. The peril they faced was just as big. The lines had limped out of the war, worn to the axles. Competition from trucks, planes, and waterborne carriers, already formidable, leaped ahead. . . . High-priced packaged cargo was moving over the highways; barges and pipelines were cutting into the bulk loads—the sand, ore, oil, and coal that were once ticketed largely as rail freight. On the passenger side, the shift was even more drastic.

    [1] From "Revolution on Rails" by John A. Conway, associate editor of *Newsweek.* *Newsweek.* 46:89-94. N. 21, '55. Reprinted by permission.

The [railroads'] answer has been a decade of frenetic activity that rivals the wild years of the last century, when the empire builders hammered their way to the Pacific and in ten years stretched the nation's trackage by some 70,000 miles. The industry still runs, by and large, over the spider-web routes traced by the surveyors and speculators who opened the West. But in a very real sense, it is what the Santa Fe calls "a new railroad." It is driven by engines that are far more efficient than the almost extinct steam locomotive that set hearts pounding in man and boy only a few years ago. Radar and television, electronic eyes, brains, and hands unscramble and reassemble freight trains in its yards. Now automatic controls let one track do the work of two.

Workhorse of the postwar rail revolution has been the Diesel. This bullheaded monster, whose blatting horn has replaced the romantic wail of the whistle, is not new; the Burlington put the word into the American vocabulary with its 1934 "Zephyrs." But since 1945, the roads have laid out $3.3 billion for 20,924 new engines—and 20,456 of them are Diesels. The economics are simple. A Diesel will do as much work on $1 worth of fuel oil as a steamer of comparable power will do on $2 worth of coal. Using practically no water, the Diesel eliminated need for $50 million worth of water supply and treating paraphernalia to serve the thirsty steamers. [For a discussion of Diesels and other modern equipment see "Up from the Wood Burners," in Section I, above.]

Today the oil-driven fleet pulls almost 86 per cent of all freights and better than 88 per cent of the passenger trains. More than fifty major lines own no steam locomotives at all. . . . Nor is the Diesel the last word. Lines are now working with brand-new gas-turbine power and still more advanced engines operating on such fuels as powdered coal. On the horizon is the atomic locomotive, which Alco Products, Inc., formerly American Locomotive, and other companies are hard at work on.

Payload

The freight car fleet has been getting even more attention and, when car-handling facilities are added, even more money than the powerhouses of the railroads. . . . More billions went for new car-repair shops and electronic freight-sorting yards. . . . As part of the effort to ease the freight-car pinch, the rails have lavished brains and money on getting more mileage out of the cars they have. Even a 10 per cent speed-up of freights now rolling, the experts figure, would activate $1 billion worth of cars. That helps explain the vast yard-rebuilding program which is turning the back-breaking job of shuffling freight trains into a pushbutton operation. The new yards combine the newest and oldest forces available—gravity and electronics. (Basically, the robot yards work like this. Freights entering the yard are pushed up an artificial "hump," uncoupled, then allowed to roll into a skein of classification tracks. From his watchtower, the yardmaster presses buttons to guide the free-rolling cars automatically into new combinations, ready to roll. Robot scales weigh the cars, radar gauges their speed, automatic retarders control it. These retarders alone let a handful of operators and field men do a job that once required fifty to seventy "car riders.") These showpiece freight yards spell hard savings. The Pennsylvania, for instance, now has completed the eastbound section of its sprawling setup at Conway, Pennsylvania, near Pittsburgh. Eventually, the Pennsy figures, this $34 million yard will save it $11 million a year in operating expenses and cut long-haul freight schedules by twenty-four hours. The Southern Pacific's robot yard at Houston, Texas, is saving it $5,000 a week in car rentals, even with only part of it in service.

Besides the precious time clipped from the freight schedules, these new yards are helping to soothe another huge railroad headache—freight damage. Each year the lines pay irate shippers a cool $100 million for cargoes smashed in transit, much of it by freewheeling switchmen in the yards. The slide-rule crew on one line figured out that a loaded car, rolling at 7 miles per hour, packs the same wallop as an auto slamming into a wall at better than 340 miles per hour. In one of the Milwaukee Road's electronic yards, the delicate touch of the robots cut damage in one month to below $900, a figure railroaders still whistle at.

With that sort of return on investment, it is small wonder the roads are pouring money into these yard-building programs. The Southern Railway, with a new $14 million yard at Chattanooga, Tennessee, is laying out a $15 million replica at Atlanta, Georgia. The Seaboard Air Line has a new $7 million yard in North Carolina. . . .

The spend-to-save policy has paid off all down the line, helped keep the colossal bill for maintaining 393,000 miles of track and thousands of buildings along the lines ($1.3 billion last year) from going still higher. A couple of years ago one line put $85,000 into bulldozers, crawler-cranes, and other off-track equipment and scrapped its rail-borne steam ditchers and cranes. The drop in unit costs spelled an annual saving of $750,000. In the old days, track gangs used to crop the ends of track battered by the pounding wheels. Now rails go through a special end-hardening process at the steel mills. One expert has put the savings at $24 a mile each year—no small change for an industry with a continental network of track to worry over.

High Iron, High Finance

Thirty years ago, a fifty-mile, single-track stretch of the Missouri Pacific went on "centralized traffic control" (CTC in railroadese). One man in a central tower set signals and threw switches for the entire stretch. By 1942, more than 200 such installations controlled 2,000 miles of track; by . . . [1954] over 22,000 miles were on CTC. The savings can be enormous. One thirty-three-mile CTC setup has saved a line more than 3,000 freight-car days annually. . . . The New York Central . . . has work under way to convert the four-track mainline from Buffalo to Cleveland to CTC. Cost: $6.2 million.

While the high-iron men were out on the line, the white-collar crews in the home offices were hammering away at their own bugaboo, the sky-high debt that has ridden the caboose of most railroads since the Civil War. Getting this excess baggage into manageable size and shape has streamlined the rail operation almost as much as the new rolling stock has. The Baltimore & Ohio refinancing, for instance, was the biggest such project any railroad had ever handled without going through the bankruptcy mill.

Aside from the psychological lift, the rearrangement of rail finances has put real cash into the working till. The Rock Island put through a plan . . . to redeem $65 million in 5 per cent convertible preferred stock and at the same time to sell $62.5 million in debentures. By eliminating a preferred dividend requirement of $3,234,000 a year and substituting the interest charge on the debentures, the road saves $423,000 annually. The Milwaukee Road, in a similar maneuver, swapped 600,000 preferred shares for debentures. Result: A $1.5 million-a-year saving in income taxes. . . .

Disaster still hung over the right of way, however. The rails' share of U.S. cargo business has been dropping 1.9 per cent a year. The boom has kept up tonnages, but the lines must check the decline in their share of the market.

The competition is getting stronger by the day. . . . West Coast shipping circles are hearing talk of a new fleet of coastwise vessels that would carry anywhere from two hundred to five hundred loaded trailers—at the usual low waterborne rates. A Mobile, Alabama, shipper has announced its intention of reviving East Coast and Gulf shipping with a new fleet of roll-on, roll-off vessels.

The Diesels, automatic freight yards, robot switching, and the like, are of course part of the strategy to produce a better rail service and more business. More specific—and competitive— are the relatively new piggyback programs . . . [see "Piggyback Riding," in this section, below], new trains to recapture some of the passenger traffic from the airlines, and sales programs to bring plants and cargoes into areas along the rail right of way. President Paul E. Feucht of the North Western adds it up this way: "You've got to have volume to get gross to get net.". . .

To drum up new carloadings, the roads have worked both sides of another two-way street. Industry trekking South found lines like the Southern Railway waiting with open sidings. In the already crowded industrial East, president Joseph A. Fisher, whose Reading Railroad has been sounding the siren call for plants on the move, notes that in the first nine months . . . [of 1955] thirty-one new customers set up shop along its route.

What about passengers? Talk of passenger traffic usually sends railroaders to the wailing wall. Nonetheless, the lines are laying out hard cash to win more riders—and more contented ones. Just as the Union Pacific's streamliners helped restore romance to the railroads in the thirties, so the industry expects the new lightweight, low-level fliers to start more travelers heading toward its terminals instead of to airports or out on highways.

The New York Central has a brace of the "dream trains" in the works. . . . The Pennsylvania is set to test a couple of low-level designs, particularly for short hauls. President [James M.] Symes sees little promise in passenger business at distances over one thousand miles. "Realistically," he says, "the time element is too much of a factor in favor of air service."

Symes would get an argument from [president] Fred Gurley of the Santa Fe, whose El Capitan, rolling the 2,200 miles from Chicago to Los Angeles in 39.5 hours has been a consistent moneymaker. The Santa Fe will soon have a low-level train and will try it out in short-haul service. For long hauls, the line is now getting delivery on the first units of a new "high-level" train. Gurley's experts reason this way:

These cars, similar in height to dome cars [15.5 feet] let us put baggage storage space, larger rest rooms, and other services at the lower level so that we get twenty-eight seats more per car. For 39.5-hour trips, passengers need space to roam, to stretch out, to get a taste of the scenery.

General Motors, which pioneered one of the new trains the roads are testing, has given an idea of the dollar-and-cents thinking behind them. Dome coaches, most of them with eighty seats, now cost $2,250 a seat. Its new cars, GM says, would run $900 to $1,000 a seat in volume production.

Pruning costs and picking up new customers are simply good business, of course, but it is the avowed conviction of the railroads that they won't be able to do their job and make money at full throttle until Washington clears the tracks. The government, they insist, must lift the restrictions clamped on when the robber barons rode the rails and when "the public be damned" was a watchword. This may, in part, explain why the roads still go to such lengths to build up passenger traffic, while bemoaning deficits. A pleased passenger means a voter who will lend an ear when the railroads plead their case on Capitol Hill. . . .

Loosening of what railroaders call the "shackles" of regulation is not all the help the railroads feel they should have. Taxes have always been a sore point, with the rails contending that the trucks were rolling tax-paved highways and the waterborne inland carriers were using a right of way built by God and the government. The railroad argument is that while they are staggering under a huge tax load, they are still paying to keep up their own roads. Besides, they point out, their competitors pay far less in taxes. [See "Taxing the Railroads out of Business," in Section II, above.]. . .

Without a helping hand from Congress, railroaders can see no Eldorado ahead, but the future is not exactly gloomy. With the U.S. industrial machine roaring, the rails will be busier than ever. In the next decade, population should climb to nearly 190 million; gross national product should pile up to $535 billion. The national freight traffic by that time, rail men figure, will stand at a mountainous 1.5 trillion ton miles. The Pennsy's president Symes thinks the industry will have to spend more than double the $10 billion laid out in the last ten years to meet . . . the demand.

Even if the rails' share of this huge traffic continues to dwindle at the current rate, the freight lines will carry 17 per cent more in 1965 than they did . . . [in 1955]. If the railroads reverse that curve—and Symes predicts that rails will carry 55 per cent instead of 51 per cent of the load by 1965—the "new railroad" will have to be built all over again—and railroaders will be singing while they build.

FREIGHT WARS AND FREIGHT RATES [2]

Under Federal regulation, U.S. freight transportation has become what heavily regulated industries tend to become, a kind of state-run cartel.

The familiar European cartel was an association of companies that controlled production and prices in order to prevent the "abuses" and "excesses" of competition; and the big objection to cartels, of course, was that they always tended to and often did restrain production, productivity, and progress. The American economy is based on the belief that any such restraint is bad, and the American people have written that belief into the law of the land.

Yet the fact is that government regulation has not only caused inefficient carriers to be subsidized and promoted at the expense of efficient carriers, it has given nonregulated carriers unfair advantage over regulated carriers, and so has encouraged the maintenance of a larger transportation plant than the nation needs. It has intensified the natural inertia of the rule-bound railroads. Above all, it has kept them from competing for traffic that they could haul profitably and economically, and so has forced them to maintain higher rates than they would otherwise have maintained. Government regulation, in brief, has compelled the nation to pay more for freight transportation that it should.

And Americans spend more on transportation than on any other commodity or service—upwards of $75 billion a year when private autos and all that is needed to run them are counted in. To be sure, a considerable part of this colossal outlay, since it is devoted to personal transportation, represents an end in itself, a service or pastime that people enjoy. But nearly half of this $75-billion-plus worth of transportation is spent in moving

[2] From "The Great U.S. Freight Cartel," by Gilbert Burck, member of the Board of Editors of *Fortune* magazine. *Fortune*. 55:102-5+. Reprinted by special permission from the January 1957 issue of *Fortune* magazine. © 1957 by Time Inc.

goods around in the course of getting them made and distributed, and the efficiency with which the job is performed profoundly affects the price of everything.

The most important part of the nation's commercial and industrial transportation outlay is the $27 billion or so that U.S. business spends to transport intercity freight by rail, truck, oil pipelines, internal waterways, and airways. It is fair to say that the U.S. intercity freight-transportation system is the world's most efficient chiefly because it is the only large system that is entirely owned and operated by private interests trying to make a profit out of it. But it is also fair to say that the U.S. freight-transportation system today is much less efficient than it could be. This is so because the system is regulated by a government whose freight-transportation policies, embodied in the much-patched Interstate Commerce Act, are a hodgepodge of obsolete and often contradictory ideas. And the administrator of this act, the venerable Interstate Commerce Commission, has found itself unable to exploit or even define adequately the role of competition in transportation. Thus it has failed to make transportation productivity a prime or even major goal of regulation. The fact that the ICC has led an honorable and often useful life does not exempt it from the devastating criticism that under its wide and benign umbrella there has been more and more room for anyone with a persuasive voice, whether shipper, carrier, patron, politician, or farmer, but less and less room for the interest of the nation as a whole. . . .

In a reasonably free economy, shaped significantly by market forces, one would expect the share of the total inter-city freight dollar enjoyed by any carrier to reflect that carrier's productivity. The carrier with the highest output per dollar of cost should produce ton-miles the most cheaply; and unless its competitors offer special services that it does not offer (as air freight does), it should get the business. This natural allocation of traffic, however, has not been the rule in the United States.

During the past quarter-century total intercity ton-miles (tons hauled times miles covered), including those produced by non-regulated trucks and waterway operators, have just about kept pace with physical production—despite the frequent assumption that industrial decentralization results in proportionately less transportation. Even as the physical volume of U.S. production has a little more than doubled since 1929, intercity ton-miles have risen from about 630 billion to about 1,340 billion. . . . All four of the important carriers of U.S. intercity freight—oil pipelines, waterways, truckers, and railroads—have shared this huge increase in freight volume, but they do not share the traffic today as they shared it before 1929. Let us see how the increase in their volume corresponds to their productivity.

The ton-mile volume of the oil pipelines has risen more than four times since 1929—from 54 billion to 225 billion—and their share of total intercity ton-miles has accordingly about doubled, rising from 8 per cent to 17 per cent. This gain is mainly the result of superior efficiency in rendering a very special service. Although capital investment in oil pipelines is high—$70,000 per employee, against $25,000 per employee in the railroad industry—it is this capital investment that has enabled pipelines to transport oil much more efficiently, and hence more cheaply, than other overland carriers; and appropriately, they have made a lot of money doing so.

For the internal waterways the increased share of the total freight business is not so easy to justify. Internal-waterway carriers fall under two distinct headings: those on the Great Lakes, whose productivity is colossal, and those on rivers and canals, whose productivity is conjectural. The Great Lakes carriers are largely contract and captive, devoted to carrying bulk ore, coal, limestone, and grain, and since 1929 they have shown very little increase in ton-mile volume and an actual decrease in their share of the national ton-mile volume. Their revenues, on which they earn handsome profits, average only 0.2 cents a ton-mile, against 1.4 cents for the railroads and 6.5 cents for trucks. However, they perform no loading or unloading.

The river and canal carriers, by contrast, have increased their ton-miles twelve times since 1929—from 9 billion to 108 billion—and their share of total intercity ton-miles from 2 per cent to 8 per cent. But these carriers, more than any of the others,

owe their very existence to the fact that their rights-of-way have
been and still are heavily subsidized by the Federal Government.
The construction and maintenance of river and canal channels is
the job of the Army Engineers, who for more than a century
have been dredging and keeping waterways open in the name of
national defense and flood control. And the selection of channels to be dredged and improved provides Congress with its
No. 1 opportunity for porkbarreling, which has resulted in outlays by the Federal Government alone, since World War II, of
perhaps $2 billion for waterway improvement and maintenance.
State and local governments have also shelled out untold millions
on waterways.

Only a few years ago many students of transportation believed
that barge-line efficiency, measured by total costs including capital and maintenance costs assumed by the government, was below
land-transport efficiency. Ever since World War II, however,
river and canal carriers, and particularly those on the Mississippi
River system, have been booming. Adequately financed and ag-
gressively managed, they have improved their efficiency with
larger barges and more powerful towboats, and they have increased their ton-miles by 300 per cent since 1946, and by more
than 100 per cent since 1950. The question has arisen, as a matter of fact, whether river and canal carriers are not handling
enough traffic efficiently enough to bear the cost of the government's outlays on waterway improvements, and the Hoover
Commission has already proposed user charges based on maintenance and operating costs.

The trouble is that nobody knows how efficient the barge industry really is, and the operators themselves are laying low
and offering as little information as possible. Only about 10
per cent of river and canal traffic is under ICC regulation; exempt is traffic hauled by private carriers and by bulk carriers
handling no more than three commodities. And the law accords
regulated waterway carriers special consideration. Section 305
(c) of the Interstate Commerce Act provides that the ICC, in
approving water carriers' rates, can disregard the effect of these
rates on rail competition; on the other hand, the ICC has not

let railroads make rates that would drive the waterway carriers out of business. By their own admission, many waterway operators find themselves in a contradictory if profitable position. They argue that they offer "inherently cheaper transportation" and should be allowed to price their product below their competitors', but they also argue that they cannot price their product "competitively" if they are charged their share of government-financed overhead.

The Great Freight Paradox

The economic contradictions of U.S. freight transportation show up no more strikingly than in the relative performance of trucks and railroads, which together roll up slightly more than two thirds of all intercity ton-miles. Ton-miles produced by intercity truckers have increased no less than 1,100 per cent since 1929. . . . How much the truckers' dollar volume has increased is impossible to estimate with any precision. For only about a third of all intercity truck ton-miles are produced by ICC-regulated trucks. The rest are rolled up by "private" vehicles (those owned and operated by companies for their own use) and by carriers exempt from ICC regulation. None of these report their revenues or costs to the ICC. Assuming that the ton-mile costs and imputed revenues of the "private" and exempt carriers are roughly equal to those of ICC regulated trucks, dollar volume of intercity truckers has risen from an estimated $375 million in 1929 to an estimated $16 billion in 1956, or from 7 per cent to 59 per cent of total intercity freight dollar volume.

Ton-miles produced by railroads, by contrast, have actually declined from 72 per cent to 49 per cent of the total. In absolute terms, they have risen 45 per cent—from 450 billion ton-miles in 1929 to 655 billion in 1956. And railroad dollar volume has less than doubled, rising from $4.9 billion to an estimated $9 billion. Consequently the railroads' share of estimated total dollar volume has declined from 87 per cent to 34 per cent.

For an additional 200 billion railroad ton-miles, in other words, the nation paid an additional $4 billion. But for an additional 200 billion truck ton-miles, the nation probably paid

more than $15 billion.   So today the railroads are producing
more than two and a half times as many ton-miles as the truckers,
but are getting about $7 billion less for doing so. Plainly enough,
railroads are producing ton-miles more cheaply than the trucks.
But plainly, too, they have been unable to get the business to
which lower costs alone would seem to entitle them. Before trying to unlock this paradox, let us look more closely at the productivity of trucks and railroads.

It is one of the ironies of government regulation that the
ICC, which has the final responsibility for interstate freight
rates, has been unable to get elementary statistics about the trucking industry as a whole, to say nothing of relevant information
about its efficiency. Because Congress has so far refused to appropriate money for a transportation census, the ICC doesn't
even know how many of the 10 million trucks on the road are
in interstate commerce. It guesses they number about 750,000,
but the ICC does not get very close even to these 750,000.
Directly regulated by it are only 18,000 carriers operating the
300,000 trucks that account for about a third of all intercity
highway ton-miles. What they haul the ICC knows not, even
though it has been trying to find out for years. Many are small
operators that do not themselves compile the information the
ICC asks them for.

The big truckers, however, do report enough data to the ICC
to justify reasonable inferences about truck efficiency on the
basis of annual revenue ton-miles (ton-miles of revenue freight)
per employee. Some truck companies whose runs are long,
notably Pacific Intermountain Express, operating between Chicago
and the West Coast, roll up as many as 270,000 revenue ton-
miles a year per employee. Other truckers, even big ones, are
lucky to achieve 100,000. All told, the average efficiency of
trucks in interstate commerce may be estimated at about 160,000
revenue ton-miles per employee per year; and the efficiency of
private and exempt trucking is probably lower.

Railroads, by contrast, average 765,000 revenue ton-miles annually per freight employee (based on ICC cost allocation). As
in the trucking industry, however, output varies greatly among
the carriers. Some railroads turn in fewer than 300,000 annual

revenue ton-miles per employee, while output of some coal-carrying roads is more than 1 million annual revenue ton-miles per employee. But on the average, railroad productivity, expressed in terms of ton-miles per employee, is about five times that of truck productivity. And the disparity probably would be even greater if expressed in terms of ton-miles per employee *hour*. For a large percentage of railroad employees are paid on a mileage basis, and do not work a full eight hours a day, whereas most commercial-trucking employees probably do.

A ton-mile-per-employee comparison of efficiency, of course, is incomplete because it takes no account of costs other than wages—for example, the railroads' capital investment, which is about ten times as much per employee as the average truck line's capital investment. But because railroads depreciate capital goods more slowly and roll up more ton-miles per employee, railroad freight labor plus capital costs average about .7 cents a ton-mile, or less than a fifth as much as the truckers' 3.8 cents. This relationship is also reflected in total average costs, which are about 1.2 cents a ton-mile for railroads and close to 6.4 cents a ton-mile for trucks.

Everybody's Trucking

Then how have intercity truckers increased their share of the traffic so handsomely, while railroads have lost so much of theirs? Trucks, of course, are more efficient than railroads on short hauls and for many less-than-carload hauls, and they can undercut railroad rates and still make money on such hauls. Furthermore, part of the intercity truck volume—nobody knows how much—consists of goods carried to and from business establishments without rail service.

What is more important, a truck ton-mile is often different from a railroad ton-mile. There is growing demand for the kind of transportation supplied by trucks, even though it may be less efficient and more expensive on a ton-mile basis. For the American economy is steadily becoming more and more a fast-turnover economy. As industry becomes at once more diversified and dispersed, traffic tends to move in smaller shipments over shorter distances, and the kind of speed and convenience supplied by trucks becomes worth extra money. That is one reason many companies find it advantageous to operate their own intercity trucks. Producers and distributors, for example, do not have to call on someone else to move their goods, and can fit their transport schedules to production schedules.

Yet the differences between truck and railroad ton-miles probably do not begin to account for the fact that trucks have increased their share of intercity traffic from 3 to 18 per cent while the railroads' share dropped from 72 to 49 per cent. The railroads have clearly lost a great deal of business to trucks, even as they have lost some to internal waterways, because their prices are too high. And why, if their costs are so low, have their prices been so high?

That Old Rate Structure

The reason is the railroad rate structure, which was built up over the years not on a *cost-of-service* but on a *value-of-service* basis. Right from the start, railroads tried to create all the business they could, and they naturally adopted a policy of charging what the traffic would bear. A difference of 2 or 3 cents a ton-mile in the rate on dresses, for example, made practically no difference in the retail price of a single dress hauled five hundred miles. But a difference of 2 mills a ton-mile in the price charged for hauling coal meant $1 on each ton of coal hauled five hundred miles. So, "to encourage the free movement of all commodities," railroads set high ton-mile rates on high-priced products like food, apparel, tobacco, and spirits, and low rates on heavy bulk commodities like coal, ore, sand, gravel, and cement (on all of which, however, they usually made money). By and large, this system of rate making worked very well for railroads while they had a virtual monopoly of transportation. Most economic historians adopt the view that it also worked well for the nation, since it set relatively low rates on important bulk commodities that built the country's industries.

When new competition came along, this monopolistic rate structure was easy game for it. The railroads had priced far above cost precisely the things the new competitors could haul most conveniently. What is more, the railroads' new competitors, and particularly the truckers, although they described themselves as common carriers, were at best quasi-common carriers. A freight common carrier, ideally, offers to take anything the other carriers take, and shares alike in the high and low-profit business. The new so-called common carriers, because they took only the business they wanted or were equipped to handle, competed selectively. They rolled off with the high-profit traffic.

An ordinary business, finding itself in such a situation, would revise its prices to reflect costs more accurately. Why didn't the railroads revise their rates? For one thing, they were too set in their ways and too accustomed to getting along on momentum to take up the cudgels. They even missed the chance to get into trucking themselves back in the days before it was regulated. And later on, instead of pitching their case on superior efficiency, railroads tried to persuade the competition to play the game like gentlemen.

For another thing, there was the railroad rate structure itself. It governs the location and very life of many industries, and it cannot be altered drastically and summarily without harming a great many people. And finally there was the venerable, painstaking, hard-working, honorable, but unimaginative and economically diffident Interstate Commerce Commission. Interpreting its congressional mandate (as well as many court decisions on rates) as a charge to preserve the existing proportions of the railroad rate structure, indeed, regarding almost any change as drastic and summary, the ICC tended to allow all carriers, no matter what their productivity, a "fair share" of the available traffic.

The ICC Takes Over

As a matter of fact, the Interstate Commerce Commission was never dedicated *primarily* to the fostering of an efficient transportation system. It was set up in 1887 to protect the nation both against railroad monopoly and railroad competition. The overbuilt, voraciously competitive railroads were giving handsome rebates to big shippers and shippers with a choice of carriers, and exploiting shippers who had no choice. The ICC's early powers were limited and punitive, consisting, in the main, of the right to cancel rates that were "unreasonable, unjust, or discriminatory," and to see to it that carriers did not pool traffic and did not charge more per ton-mile for a short haul than for a long haul over the same line. Such regulation, at the time, was undeniably necessary.

But it was not long before the ICC was doing more than preventing abuses. Amendments to the Interstate Commerce Act gave it power to fix maximum, minimum, and exact rates. The amendment of 1920 handed it the responsibility for building up a strong, prosperous transportation system. This amendment also handed the ICC the impossible job of drawing up a railroad-consolidation plan that would promote efficiency without disturbing existing competitive relationships and channels of trade—which is about like telling a manager to cut costs without reducing his money payments to anyone.

Later amendments did nothing to increase the ICC's concern for efficiency. The Motor Carrier Act of 1935 put motor carriers under ICC jurisdiction, and the amendment of 1940 did the same for some of the internal-waterway operators. Numbed by years of regulation, the railroads believed more regulation was the answer to the new competition, and rejoiced in the development.

The railroads are doubtless ruing their shortsightedness. For the Amendment of 1940, which attempted to lay down some general principles for U.S. transportation, could not have been worded more ambiguously by a cartel lawyer. It called for "fair and impartial regulation" and for the recognition and preservation of the "inherent advantages" of each form of transportation —which sounds fine but can be, and indeed has been, interpreted as a mandate to the ICC, in effect, to allocate traffic on the basis of the "service characteristics" of the competition. The act also called for "the fostering of sound economic conditions in transportation and among the several carriers and the elimination of unjust discriminations and advantages"—which also sounds fine but has been interpreted as a directive to help any and all transportation make money. And although the act slipped in the usual references to "safe, adequate, and economical service," it said nothing specific about efficiency or productivity.

Efficient transportation is also handicapped by the way the law compels the ICC to operate. The ICC follows the procedure of a common-law court, and combines the functions of an administrative body and an expert tribunal. In the days when railroads had a monopoly of transportation, this combination worked all right, but even ICC commissioners began to argue that the common-law-court system ought to be modified.

Modified signficantly it has not been. A proposed rate change, for example, must be filed thirty days before it goes into effect, so that interested parties may have a chance to consider it. The ICC may suspend the rate on its own authority or, if somebody files a protest, send the proposed rate to its suspension board. If the rate is suspended, the case is assigned to an ICC examiner, who may hold hearings. The examiner at length files his report and an order is issued disposing of the case, but if anybody complains, the case can be appealed to the commission and later to the courts. Since arguments must be scheduled forty-five days ahead of time, a case can drag on for more than a year. In 1946, for example, it took nearly a whole year to grant the railroads a general rate increase, and in 1947 it took eleven months to dispose of a rate case. The ICC was recently reorganized, it is true, and it has sped up many of its processes. But the mandate and the basic processes remain.

That, incidentally, is one of the reasons railroad consolidation has languished. Although the urge to merge has not been a distinguishing characteristic of railroad managers, some owners and managers today would like to consolidate. But they feel that any *effective* plan is almost automatically doomed because the ICC must give attentive ear to all the special interests that might be hurt or inconvenienced.

The Unsupervised

The ICC is also handicapped by the fact that it hasn't a sufficiently broad jurisdiction to do a thorough job of regulation. Probably an even smaller minority of water carriers than truck carriers, for example, reports to the ICC. And it never has been able to get a useful volume of figures from them, to say nothing of regulating them effectively. Contract truck carriers, which as their name implies, undertake to haul only freight contracted for, are under little supervision even in interstate commerce. They are everywhere undermining both motor and rail common carriers by making *ad hoc* rates the way railroads did in the days before 1887.

A large proportion of so-called private truck carriers, too, are actually engaging in for-hire carriage by various dodges, such as temporarily transferring ownership of a cargo to the operator, or by surreptitiously loading up with other than the owner's freight on return trips. And there are the carriers of farm products, which are legislatively exempt from ICC regulation. Owing to liberal court interpretations of what constitutes farm produce, these carriers are hauling such things as commercially frozen and processed foods free of regulation.

But what is much more important than the defects in regulatory machinery is the fact that the ICC feels compelled to stick to the principle that competing carriers should be assured "participation in the traffic," and that rates need not be based primarily on costs because they should not be lower than "competitively necessary." . . .

The "competitively fair" concept is of course both unfair and uneconomic. Pipelines have put railroads out of the petroleum-hauling business because they do the job more efficiently and cheaply. It would be absurd to argue that pipeline rates should be raised so that railroads could share the business; yet railroads are forced to set rates on the principle that traffic must be shared with other carriers.

One underlying trouble is that nobody has yet developed a good cost-finding formula for rail freight, i.e., a formula that determines when a rate, assuming it will attract a given amount of traffic, will cover the carrier's out-of-pocket expenses plus a reasonable share of overhead expenses. The railroads, at least until recently, have contented themselves with grumbling about the inadequacies of ICC data, and only a few of them have even begun to develop cost-research techniques.

Toward a New Policy

All this may be changing. Responsible opinion, since World War II, has been gathering behind the proposition that U.S. transportation policies badly need revising. In 1949, for example, the Brookings Institution published a very good book, *National Transportation Policy*, by Charles Dearing and Wilfred Owen, who argued that the whole freight rate structure would have to be changed from the value-of-service to the cost-of-service principle.

In July 1954, President Eisenhower appointed a "Cabinet" Committee—so-called because it included several Cabinet members—to examine U.S. transportation policy. The committee's report, unanimously adopted and published in April 1955, was a drastic but on the whole a fair document. It sketched in the background quickly—competition in transportation was now pervasive, it said, but competitive forces were tightly reined, and government regulation prevented the most economical use of transportation plant. The report argued that more reliance should be put on competitive forces, that the prime criterion of a rate should be the cost of providing the service and not the rate's effect on other carriers and finally, that minimum rates should be fixed by the ICC only when proposed rates were clearly non-compensatory in terms "of the direct ascertainable cost of providing the service." So long as one carrier could show that it would make something on a proposed rate (and so long as the proposed rate was not unjust or discriminatory), that rate should stand.

The report also proposed (1) that Congress put the burden of proof on a competing carrier asking for the suspension of a proposed rate, (2) that a rail or water carrier be allowed, without prior ICC approval, to make a lower ton-mile rate for a long haul than for a shorter haul over the same route (though the published rate would still be subject to suspension after a complaint); (3) that Congress let carriers make volume or trainload rates; (4) that Congress empower the ICC to override state authorities in such matters as the abandonment of railroad passenger service. . . .

Meantime, the Interstate Commerce Act is not only driving traffic into uneconomic channels, it is depriving management of its prerogatives, and the nation of lower freight costs. It is forcing the ICC to become an excellent example of how a government agency set up to protect the people can do the people harm. What the act needs is the kind of amendment proposed in the Cabinet report. The only way to put freight transportation on an economic basis is to let productivity, manifesting itself through more freedom in rate making, play a larger role in allocating the transportation resources of the nation.

PIGGYBACK RIDING [3]

On every business day of the week, nearly two thousand truck trailers—carrying everything from machines to shoes— are loaded bodily aboard railroad flat-cars for long-distance hauling to destinations all over the country.

This system of trucking by rail, called "piggybacking," is catching on so fast with shippers, truckers and railroads that many authorities will tell you it promises a revolution in the movement of freight.

The effects of this growth in piggybacking, in the years ahead, could touch just about everybody. For motorists on the highways, it means some relief from a major headache: the growing thousands of huge trailer trucks crowding the roads and adding to traffic hazards. . . . For the railroads, it offers new hope of halting the loss of freight tonnage. Few see it yet as a full answer to rail problems, but, in the words of one official, piggybacking is the "brightest spot" in the railroad picture.

Today, fifty railroads, including all the major lines, offer piggyback service. These railroads, operating in fifty states, account for 86 per cent of all tracks, though piggybacking is not yet available in all the places served. In just five years piggybacking volume has multiplied 2.5 times. In 1959, piggy-

[3] From " 'To Market, To Market . . .' by Truck on a Train." *U.S. News & World Report.* 48:100-2. F. 1, '60. Reprinted from *U.S. News & World Report,* an independent weekly news magazine published at Washington. Copyright 1960 United States News Publishing Company.

back carloadings reached 415,000.   Many of these cars carried more than one trailer.

Now the shippers and railroads are pushing piggyback service into new fields—automobiles, the U.S. mail, fresh fruits, gasoline.   This signals even faster growth.   As just one developing example, look at the way piggybacking is catching hold in the automobile industry. . . . Chrysler Corporation cars are brought to Chicago from Detroit by regular auto-transport trailers.   These trailers are then loaded on flatcars of the Milwaukee Road for shipment to Spokane, Washington.   After arrival, the trailers are hooked up to trucks again and deliveries are made to auto dealers in Washington and Oregon.   Railroad officials estimate the piggyback operation cuts transit time from Detroit to Spokane by five days. . . .

The Chevrolet Division of General Motors has been using piggyback for more than a year.   Other GM divisions are thinking about using this service.   American Motors plans a test run of autos by piggyback from St. Louis to Dallas "in the near future."

Hauling mail by piggyback has been started . . . by four major railroads in eastern and midwestern states.   A number of other railroads are now thinking about getting into the field.

Postal officials say that piggybacking a truck trailer saves time over shipping mail in a railroad car, because the mail does not have to be loaded into a truck when the train pulls into a station.   The trailer can be hooked up to a truck in a matter of a few minutes.

"On the Chicago-to-Detroit run," says a Post Office official, "we figure we are saving as much as three hours.   In some towns along the route, that means mail is delivered twenty-four hours earlier than before.   The reason is that we now can get mail to some post offices in time to be sorted and given to carriers before they go out for the day."

Piggyback service has also moved into agricultural commodities.   The Missouri Pacific Railroad is now rushing fruits and vegetables in specially equipped cars from the Rio Grande Valley of Texas to the St. Louis market area.   The United

States Agriculture Department predicts that more and more farm products will be moving by piggyback in coming months.

Increasing demands for this new service are coming at a time when the field is already booming. . . . In 1955 some 32 railroads handled an average of 3,200 piggyback carloads a week. In 1959 50 railroads loaded an average of 8,000 cars a week. Railroad officials expect continued rapid growth in piggybacking.

Daniel P. Loomis, president of the Association of American Railroads, says: "Half of the nation's railroad freight may one day move in loaded highway trailers and containers piggyback on freight cars." Piggyback carloadings now amount to less than 2 per cent of total carloadings. . . . W. P. Kennedy, president of the Brotherhood of Railroad Trainmen, says of piggybacking: The potential is so great that this modern method of moving freight promises a major revolution in transportation. It gives the shipper faster long-haul service with all the advantages of door-to-door delivery." . . .

There are five basic piggyback plans—two or more of which may be offered by the same railroad:

Plan 1. The railroad charges a trucking company for hauling its trailers. The trucker saves on gasoline, drivers' wages and ton-mile highway taxes, and he avoids highway restrictions on the size and weight of trailers. Eighteen railroads offer this service, according to government estimates.

Plan 2. The railroad hauls its own truck trailers. Forty-one railroads operate this kind of piggybacking.

Plan 3. Under this plan, used by twenty railroads, the railroad provides a flatcar for a trailer owned by a shipper or a freight forwarder. A freight forwarder assembles relatively small shipments of goods from manufacturers and other shippers and sends them in full flatcar loads.

Plan 4. Both the trailer and the flatcar are owned by the shipper or freight forwarder and the railroad simply does the hauling. A dozen railroads offer this plan.

Plan 5. Under this arrangement, used by only three rail-roads, joint rail-truck rates are set up to cover freight shipment by highway and rail.

The growth of piggybacking under these various plans has brought a number of problems. The major one: a lack of standard equipment.

The Public Affairs Institute, a private research organization, concluded in a study of piggybacking . . . that the lack of standardization will hinder the growth of piggyback service:

Much of the equipment is specialized and prevents one railroad's use of another's equipment. In the shipment of fresh fruits and vegetables, for example, the lack of facilities on connecting railroads to handle piggyback equipment of certain types holds back piggyback expansion.

Some carriers still operate one-trailer flatcars, where the preponderance of new cars seem to be the longer two-trailer type. . . . Some progress has been made. . . . But, for the most part, the problem of standardization in equipment . . . has not been solved.

The Interstate Commerce Commission, in an annual report released in . . . [1959] warned: "The lack of standardization in piggybacking . . . is daily becoming a more serious problem." The ICC claims that some railroads already have had to adopt more than one system in order to handle piggyback shipments with other railroads. . . .

[Most trailers now ride standard flatcars but these are far from ideal; they will accommodate only one trailer and a trailer on wheels mounted on an ordinary flatcar is too high to clear tunnels and bridges on many eastern railroads. To reduce height and increase carrying capacity, three types of cars have been developed especially for piggybacking and each manufacturer hopes his will be the "standard" equipment of the future. One is the Clejan car, named for its French designer, Deodat Clejan, and made by the General American Transportation Corporation for use with trailers and shipping containers manufactured by the Fruehauf Trailer Company. It is distinguished by a steel center beam down the length of the car on which a trailer rides on special caster wheels attached upon loading and detached upon unloading. This beam carries the entire weight of the trailer and the trailer's own wheels, to reduce clearance height, are contained in troughs on either side. Shipping containers, with similar caster wheels attached, can be loaded onto this beam as readily as trailers. The second type of piggyback car is made by American Car & Foundry Division of ACF Industries and is known as the ACF hitch. This is simply a folding stanchion that can be attached to either standard or special flatcars; when a trailer is spotted above it the hitch can be raised to hook to the trailer at the place where it is ordinarily attached to the tractor that pulls it on the highway. The ACF hitch is easily installed on ordinary flatcars to convert them to trailer use but low clearance is obtained only if they are installed on specially built, low-slung flatcars. The third is a side-loading car developed by the New York Central Railroad and called Flexi-Van. Its distinguishing feature is a turntable onto which the trailer is backed by its tractor. When the tractor pulls away the turntable swings the trailer body into position for the trip. Principal advantages are that the car needs no ramp for loading and a trailer can be placed anywhere on a train without breaking it up to load from the end of the car.—Ed.]

Difficulties with different types of piggyback equipment led to the creation of Trailer Train Company of Haverford, Pennsylvania, several years ago. This company has a pool of more than three thousand piggyback cars which can be used interchangeably by the eighteen railroads and one freight forwarder who jointly own the company.

Summing it all up, most transportation people think that equipment eventually will be made standard and that piggybacking will take over a growing share of the nation's freight hauling.

THE LONG VOYAGE HOME [4]

Into the Seaboard railroad yards at Jacksonville, Florida, the big Diesel tugged a long file of boxcars bearing the insignia of a dozen different railroads: Santa Fe, Chicago & North-

---

[4] From "The Case of the Wandering Freight Car," article by William D. Bien, journalist and magazine writer. *Reader's Digest.* 68:181-2. F. '56. Reprinted by permission.

western, New York Central. . . . In the middle, Seaboard Car 23315 rumbled by, home at last.

Almost nineteen months before, 23315 had left Seaboard's yard at Hopewell, Virginia, with a load of pulpwood, beginning an amazing odyssey that took it twice across the country, through forty-one states, over the rails of eighty-seven railroad lines.

It got a new pair of wheels at Wesleyville, Pennsylvania, while serving the New York Central. Western Pacific put on two new brake shoes in Sacramento, California, Northern Pacific replaced another in Tacoma, Washington, and the Spokane, Portland & Seattle Railway replaced four sets of wheels in Pasco, Washington. These repairs cost Seaboard $350, but offsetting that was the $1,200 that the car earned in rental fees. For 23315, like all the other 1,830,000 freight cars owned by U.S. railroads, rents for $2.40 a day whenever it is on a "foreign" line (except when laid up for repairs). [The 1960 rate is $2.88.—Ed.]

These nomads of the rails range across the land from one ocean to another, visiting Canada and Mexico, even crossing by ferry to Cuba. One day they may rumble through New England with a docile milk train, and the next go screeching across country behind a hot-shot locomotive bound for San Francisco. Who has not wondered, while watching a string of freight cars clatter past, how the railroads ever unscramble them and get them back home?

The answer lies in rules administered by the Car Service Division of the Association of American Railroads. Whenever a freight car's job is done, the rules say, it must be headed back in the general direction of home by way of the railroads that hauled it when full.

During all of 23315's shuttling journey, Seaboard knew where it was, every mile of the way. The secret is the "interchange report." Within a few minutes after it moved from one line to another, telegraphic relays at the junction began clicking. The agent for the receiving line sent a report to the car-accounting division of his road. The agent for the line the car left did the same thing. These reports were relayed to Seaboard.

One reason for the careful plotting of a car's course is the per diem rate. . . . Railroads are careful to get "foreign" cars off to other lines at junction points before 11:59 P.M., the appointed hour for the application of another rental fee. On a railroad which has several hundred junctions with other lines along its system, failures to meet the deadline at each junction point can roll up vast excess rentals in a year.

Bill Duke, boss of Chesapeake & Ohio's highly mechanized car-accounting division in Richmond, Virginia, says, "We've never lost a car." More than one hundred employees keep track of "Chessie's" 87,000 cars and the 18,000 "foreign" cars that are usually rolling on its five-thousand-mile system.

Duke showed how the car-accounting office can find out the location, destination, load and even the time schedule for any car on the system by lightning-fast decoding in business machines. He offered to "pull" any car that had been on C&O's lines in the past three years. I asked for Seaboard's 23315.

In a couple of minutes he was back with the record of the fifteen days 23315 had traveled the C&O in its wanderings. It showed, among other things, that in Freeport, New York, where 23315 had delivered a load of bolts, the rule about returning the car in the direction of the Seaboard had been forgotten. From there 23315 had been sent on to Aurora, Minnesota. As one veteran railroader said, "Theory and practice occasionally are two different things—particularly with new boxcars. Every road wants those, rules or no rules."

So that morning in Jacksonville when 23315 ground to a shrill stop, showing off the stickers and chalk marks it had collected along the way, the Seaboard men pounced. They quieted 23315 with a shot of grease, and washed the dust of California from its wheels. A thousand miles up the line, in Norfolk, the car-accounting division already was figuring the earnings.

What happened then to 23315? Well, take a look for yourself at the next freight that rolls by. Maybe you'll see it.

RAILROAD LABOR AND LABOR RELATIONS [5]

The Railroad Brotherhoods are the acme of conservative American trade unionism. Although the history of railroad unionism has been colored by . . . violent strikes . . . and a demand for the nationalization of the railroad industry, generally the Brotherhoods have appeared nonmilitant and willing to cooperate with management. The lack of militancy and cooperative attitude are based solidly on a pragmatic policy of getting "more and more" for their members and preserving job control. The Brotherhoods' method for achieving goals is the strike threat followed by quiet, but very effective, political action.

Railroad workers organized in the 1860's and 1870's to deal collectively with the problems of hazardous employment, long hours and low wages. . . . [Between 1880 and 1893 four large Brotherhoods emerged as the leading representatives of railroad labor and have subsequently been known as the Big Four. They are: the Brotherhood of Locomotive engineers, representing engineers or motormen in both road and yard service; Brotherhood of Locomotive Firemen and Enginemen, representing firemen and hostlers and their helpers in both road and yard service; Order of Railway Conductors, representing road conductors and assistant road conductors; Brotherhood of Railroad Trainmen, representing the road train baggagemen and brakemen. A fifth large union is the Switchmen's Union of North America, organized in 1894 and representing, on most roads, the yard conductors (or foremen), yard brakemen (or helpers) and switchtenders. Efforts in the early years of railroad unionism to recruit all railroad workers into an all-embracing labor organization called the Knights of Labor were unsuccessful, as was an attempt in 1894 to organize all railroad workers into a single comprehensive union known as the American Railway Union.—Ed.]

In 1900 American railroads were frequently one-track systems. Operating employees were paid by the "trip," the month, or the day. Because of the necessity for yielding right of way,

[5] From "Railroad Brotherhoods: Special Treatment," article by Edward D. Wickersham, associate professor and chairman of the Department of Management at the University of Detroit and author of *The Practice of Collective Bargaining*. *Current History*. 27:7-12. Jl. '54. Reprinted by permission.

sixteen hours of continuous duty was not uncommon. The one-track system produced a personal form of exploitation in low hourly wages and the social hazard of accident proneness due to fatigue. The Big Four dealt with both problems.

A major function of the infant Brotherhoods was provision for accident benefits. Donations for distressed members and widows were given before collective bargaining was begun. For seventy years, the Brotherhoods have administered insurance programs for their members. Probably the first evidence of the basic conservatism of the Brotherhoods was the emphasis on these insurance programs.

In their drive for protective labor legislation, the Brotherhoods emphasized the social consequence of accidents attributed to long hours of employment. In 1907, Senator LaFollette presented statistics to Congress showing the relationship of long working hours to railroad accidents. In the same year the first Federal law was passed to limit the number of work hours for railroad workers. The Hours of Service Act of 1907 provided that operating employees must be relieved for a ten-hour period after sixteen hours of work.

The Adamson Act of 1916 is a monument to the Brotherhoods' political persuasiveness. In March 1916, the Big Four Brotherhoods presented a uniform demand for the eight-hour day to all American railroads. Their demand called for a standard day of eight hours or one hundred miles and time and one half for overtime. Negotiations between the Brotherhoods and the carriers were broken off in June 1916. The breakdown of negotiations was followed by a strike vote.

The Chamber of Commerce of the United States sought to avert the nation-wide strike by asking Congress to direct the Interstate Commerce Commission to investigate wages and hours of railroad employees. President Wilson appealed to the carriers and unions. He was answered by a strike call to become effective on Labor Day, 1916. The Brotherhoods refused to arbitrate. The Adamson Act, which provided for a standard work day of eight hours, was passed on September 5, 1916, and signed by the President. The railroads contested the constitutionality of the law.

Once again the Brotherhoods prepared for a nation-wide strike. The Supreme Court weighed the evidence and concluded the law was not in conflict with the Constitution on the very day which the Brotherhoods had chosen for their strike.

The Adamson Act did much more than protect the safety of the railroad crews, passengers and freight. It incorporated the "dual system" of pay into law. The "dual system" of pay provides for a basic day's wage for a given number of miles traveled or for a period of time on duty. Under the Adamson Act one-hundred miles of travel, accomplished in eight hours or less, entitled the railroad worker to a basic day's wage. In 1916, the average railroad crew member did not cover one hundred miles in eight hours. However, the development of faster service and better scheduling has now antiquated the statutory speed. As a result, the present-day engineer frequently earns a "day's wage" in six hours or less. More important, railroad operating personnel frequently earn two days' wages in a run of 200 miles which is accomplished in eight clock hours of work. [See "Featherbedding and Make-Work," and "It's Not Featherbedding," in this section, below.]

Labor-Management Cooperation

Since 1888, the Brotherhoods had been seeking legislation which protected the "right to organize" and provided mechanisms for the peaceful settlement of disputes. The Arbitration Act of 1888 provided for voluntary arbitration of disputes. This Act was replaced by the Erdman Act in 1898. The Erdman Act provided for government mediation and conciliation services in railway labor disputes and outlawed "yellow dog" contracts. "Yellow dog" contracts made nonmembership in a labor organization a condition of continued employment. The prohibition of "yellow dog" contracts was the first step toward government protection of the "right to organize." In 1908, in the case of *Adair* v. *United States*, the Supreme Court nullified the prohibition of "yellow dog" contracts.

At the beginning of World War I, the Brotherhoods lacked (a) legal protection of the "right to organize" and (b) the firm establishment of a procedure for settling grievances arising over the interpretation of collective bargaining agreements. President Wilson took possession and control of the railroads on December 26, 1917, by executive proclamation. On February 21, 1918, the Director General of Railroads issued Order No. 8, which protected workers from discrimination because of union membership. The government further strengthened the Brotherhoods by entering national collective bargaining agreements with railroad unions. During the two years of government control the "right to organize" was an accomplished fact. The war-time establishment of regional railway boards of adjustment to settle grievances over the interpretation of collective bargaining agreements gave collective bargaining a new recognition and permanence. . . .

At the close of World War I, Congress was confronted with the old problem of regulations to prevent unfair discrimination in railroad rates, to assure a "fair" return to investors, and to encourage the peaceful settlement of labor disputes. The prospect of declining employment and wage reductions prompted the railroad unions to propose their own cure for railroad problems. Glenn W. Plumb, attorney for the railroad unions, proposed government ownership of the roads. Under the Plumb Plan, the management would be in the hands of a tripartite committee representing consumers, management, and workers. Congress rejected the advice of the railroad unions and returned the railroads to private ownership and management under the Transportation Act of 1920.

Title III of the Transportation Act of 1920 created a tripartite Railroad Labor Board to recommend settlements in labor disputes. The new law permitted the voluntary establishment of boards of adjustment to handle grievances. The "right to organize" was not given statutory protection. Neither the unions nor the carriers were satisfied with the new law.

Deep dissatisfaction with the Transportation Act of 1920 caused the Brotherhoods to support the independent candidacy of Robert M. LaFollette for President in 1924. Disappointed by the failure of the Transportation Act to establish grievance machinery, the Brotherhoods were angered by some of the appointments to the Railroad Labor Board. LaFollette's advocacy of government ownership of the railroads raised the Brotherhoods' hopes for a return of the war-time union prosperity. After the election failure, the Brotherhoods began to muster nonpartisan support for the repeal of the Transportation Act. Railroad management became their most potent political ally.

The year 1926 saw the birth of the first national labor relations statute ever formulated cooperatively by labor and management—the Railway Labor Act. The law provided for "cooling off" periods and mediation and conciliation in disputes over the terms of new agreements. Both management and labor opposed compulsory arbitration—the final determination of wages, hours, and working conditions by government edict. The law preserved the "right to strike" after extended negotiations and mediation and conciliation. To the disappointment of the unions, the 1926 law did not provide for *national* adjustment boards to handle grievance disputes. This deficiency of the law was removed by the amendments of 1934.

Railroad unions and workers weathered the Great Depression far better than their counterparts in other industries. Wage rates were not cut, but the unions allowed the carriers to deduct 10 per cent from wages during the period February 1, 1932 through June 30, 1934. On April 1, 1935, wages were restored to their January 1932 level. The Federal Emergency Railroad Transportation Act of 1933 forbade railroad mergers which would result in job-loss for the employees of the railroads.

In 1936, the railroad unions and the Class I railroads signed an agreement which provided for a 60 per cent of regular pay "displacement allowance" for workers losing their jobs as a result of mergers. The "displacement allowance" payments continued from six months to five years, depending upon the seniority of the displaced workers. The passage of the second Railroad Retirement Act of 1935 gave railroad workers the benefits of a liberalized form of Old Age and Survivors Insurance. Congress enacted an unemployment insurance act for railroad employees in 1938.

Members' Welfare

Railroad employment dropped from slightly more than 2 million in 1920 to slightly over 1 million in 1940. . . . The railroad's share of freight ton traffic in 1939 dollars declined from 87 per cent in 1920 to 63 per cent in 1940. The growth of motor trucking compensated for this decline in railroad traffic. Unemployment was further aggravated by the development of more powerful and efficient locomotives and the lengthening of trains.

The Brotherhoods met these problems through collective bargaining. They have resolutely upheld the "dual basis" of pay. . . . Since 1913, the Brotherhoods have "shared the work" by setting maximum limits on the number of miles which a member may travel in a month. The dual basis of pay minimizes the amount of work "lost" due to the advancing speed of railroad schedules, and the mileage maxima spread this work among as many employees as possible. The control of the Brotherhoods over "job opportunities" is much more comprehensive than in other industries. Professor [Sumner H.] Slichter describes it as "the principle that each and every piece of work in the operation of the railroad, no matter how minute, belongs to some particular class of employee and, in effect, is *owned* by that class."

Have the Brotherhoods done a good job of providing for the needs of their members? In 1952, the average annual wage for Brotherhood members ranged from $4,700 for yard brakemen and yard helpers to $8,100 for road freight engineers. Social Security benefits in the railroad industry are better than those in the rest of American industry. A retired railroad worker may draw a monthly annuity as high as $135. . . . Railroad workers can be certain that their unions will distribute whatever work is available on a seniority basis. The arbitrary authority of management, a major reason for all unionism, has been effectively curbed. It appears that the Brotherhoods have done an excellent job in providing for the needs of their members.

How has the effectiveness of the Brotherhoods in serving their members affected railroad management and the public? Railroad management has complained bitterly about the "make-

work" rules and the limitations on its authority to assign workers to jobs. These policies do create a substantial problem in an
industry where 40 per cent of total costs are labor costs. The
"dual basis" of pay tends to convert "variable" labor cost into
a fixed cost.

Generally, the Interstate Commerce Commission has permitted railroad rate increases to compensate for wage increases.
However, the time lag between wage increases and the granting
of a railroad rate increase places a substantial burden on the carriers. In addition, rate increases frequently mean a further loss
in traffic revenue to competing forms of transportation. No
one would argue that the Brotherhoods have made it easier for
the railroads to earn a "fair return on a fair investment." The
Brotherhoods answer the protests of management with the charge
that overcapitalization and mismanagement should not prevent
railroad workers from earning wages commensurate with their
skill and responsibility. . . .

The public interest in industrial relations in the railroad industry is probably limited to assurances that essential roalroad
service will not be interrupted by labor disputes. Two thirds of
the intercity freight traffic and half of the intercity passenger
traffic is moved by members of the Big Four. The railroad
network is the bloodstream of the American economy. Railroad
service is particularly essential in war-time. Any nation-wide
or section-wide strike would create a national emergency. However, some individual systems could be struck without crippling
the national or even regional economy. The great power of the
Brotherhoods lies in the threat of a nation-wide or area-wide
strike.

For fifteen years the Railway Labor Act was widely pro-
claimed as "ideal" labor relations legislation. It avoided compulsory arbitration and encouraged industrial peace in an essential
industry. Its "cooling off" period and emphasis on mediation and
conciliation were incorporated in the Taft-Hartley law. The
Taft-Hartley provisions on national emergency strikes bear a
striking resemblance to the "emergency boards" of the railroad
labor relations law.

Most students of labor relations have been disillusioned by recent experience with the Railway Labor Act. Since 1941 it has appeared that the Brotherhoods have had a private entrance to the White House. Three times during World War II President Roosevelt intervened in labor disputes after the unions rejected the recommendations of an emergency board and threatened to strike. Each time the unions were within their rights under the law which did *not* prohibit strikes or provide for binding awards by emergency boards.

On May 17, 1946, President Truman seized the railroads in an attempt to avert a strike threatened by the engineers and trainmen. A nation-wide strike began on May 23, 1946. President Truman appealed to the railroad workers to return to work. On May 25, the unions and the carriers reached an agreement a few minutes before President Truman asked Congress for authority to draft railroad workers. The war-time and post-war experience showed that the emergency board was not a fool-proof guarantee of industrial peace. The Brotherhoods showed a willingness to exercise their *protected* "right to strike" to achieve what they considered their legitimate demands.

The Railway Labor Act has been weakened further by the looseness of its procedures for handling grievances over the interpretation of existing collective bargaining agreements. Long delays in the disposition of grievances have irritated the Brotherhoods and their members. The present procedure is entirely permissive. Judicial review of Adjustment Board awards can be obtained *only* if the Brotherhoods apply to a District Court for enforcement. Management has no means of obtaining review other than through noncompliance with an award.

In recent years the Brotherhoods frequently have resorted to the threat of strike action to avoid the delays created by an overcrowded Adjustment Board docket and tedious court proceedings for compliance. This method of obtaining a settlement on a large bloc of cases effectively short circuits the "regular" grievance machinery. In most American industries the interpretation of the collective bargaining agreement by an arbitrator has tended to promote stability and understanding in labor relations. The present railroad procedure creates almost constant turmoil in labor relations. Whenever the unions use their *lawful* strike threat in grievance cases, the President is forced to intervene to assure a settlement.

The political "persuasiveness" of the Brotherhoods probably was not due primarily to a "pro-labor" bias of Roosevelt and Truman. The country very simply cannot stand a nation-wide railroad strike. Railroad workers, like other American workers, have job interests which are best protected by collective bargaining. Collective bargaining is effective only with a "right to strike." Destruction of the "right to strike" destroys collective bargaining.

One of the major labor problems facing the . . . [nation] is the simple question, "Can free collective bargaining be permitted to exist in the railroad industry?" The answer is not an easy one. If collective bargaining is abandoned, it must be replaced with compulsory arbitration—the determination of wages, hours and working conditions by government edict. Even in essential industries, the idea of governmental wage-fixing is not in harmony with the basic concept of a "free" economy. Under compulsory arbitration, the decisions of the market place would become *political* decisions. The abolition of the "right to strike" inevitably means the abolition of the "right to manage."

FEATHERBEDDING AND MAKE-WORK [6]

On nearly all railroads more than 50 cents of every dollar collected from freight charges and passenger fares goes out in the paychecks of employees. The human equation in the industry is the railroad man himself. He is actually something of a paradox. It would be difficult to find anywhere an employee with more loyalty to his company, more job interest and native resourcefulness, or who occupies a more secure and respected niche in the community than the railroader. On the opposite side of the coin, however, when he is represented by the monolithic power of organized labor, the rank-and-file employee is unable

[6] From "What Price Featherbedding?" article by James R. Sullivan, former locomotive engineer and train master, now vice president for traffic of the Minneapolis & St. Louis Railway. *Analysts Journal.* 15:29-33. F. '59. Reprinted by permission.

to express any concern he may personally feel for the welfare of the industry, or any individual recognition he has of the fact that obsolete and unreasonable rules in his organization's labor contract have placed a strangle hold upon the company from which he gets his livelihood.

The present difficult labor situation on the railroads has not developed overnight, nor is it the result of calculated viciousness nor intentionally destructive policies on the part of the big unions. Rather, it has grown up gradually from their strong efforts to "build fences" around particular jobs or functions and to maintain unyielding craft lines regardless of the cost to the industry. That this philosophy needs revision is evident from the fact that the total number of railroad jobs which stood at over 1.8 million in 1926 has now declined to only about 840,000. At the same time the proportion of intercity freight ton-miles handled by rail has declined by 50 per cent in a little more than a generation.

Railroad wages are generally recognized as among the highest in American industry. They have quadrupled in three decades. This, however, is not the problem. Given an effective degree of cooperation between labor and management on the railroads toward modernizing the industry's rigid and out-dated labor contracts, the carriers could readily pay substantially higher wages to their people and at the same time offer them many, many more job opportunities. At the same time the industry could turn in a far better transportation job for its patrons at much lower cost, and generate notably better returns to its investors.

Bringing to pass these very desirable benefits to all of the parties at interest—labor, management, the customer, and the investor—requires no politician's pie-in-the-sky, nor a magician's "Abracadabra." The key is found in the one word *productivity*. The railroads can be strong—and thus have a promising future to offer to employees and a worth-while return for investors—only to the degree that they are successful in increasing the number of ton-miles and passenger-miles they can produce and sell, per employee and per dollar spent for wages.

There are two distinct aspects to the idea of increased productivity per man-hour. They are often confused, either accidentally or on purpose, by people who talk and write about the subject. One is the result of replacing muscle-power with machine-power. This requires that railroad investors supply the money to buy the new machine or labor-saving device. The increased productivity generated by the machine, however, is the productivity of capital investment. It is not due to increased effort by labor. The substitution of the automatic stoker for the muscle-power of the fireman on steam locomotives made possible the hauling of larger and heavier trains. This was accomplished not through more, but actually through less effort on the part of the engine crew. The same reasoning applies to the introduction of the Diesel locomotive.

The second aspect of increased productivity, and the one in which labor is entitled to full consideration in benefiting from the results, is through reorganization of the work to permit more effective utilization of the man-hours paid for by the shipper's dollar. It is at this point that we find the conflict of ideas between management and the unions representing railroad labor.

One of our most demanding tasks in railroad management is to convince our co-workers on the labor side of the table that modernization and fundamental revision of their contracts and working agreements is essential to restoring the railroads' competitive position. We must somehow get through to these folks and make it clear that we can continue to pay high wages and employ large numbers of people only if we can increase our volume of business by greater productivity per man-hour and lower unit costs. The rewards to labor, to management, and to the investor, if we can find common cause toward this objective could be tremendous. . . .

The Feather Merchants in Action

Whenever "make-work" rules are discussed, union representatives quite understandably seek to minimize their impact upon the railroad industry and chide us for calling attention to a few isolated "horrible examples." The unfortunate part of the story is, however, that the examples are anything but isolated and when taken together constitute a tremendous financial load. "Make-work" or "feather-bed" rules are to be found in all railroads. [When Rock Island railroadmen complained about their corncob-filled caboose mattresses half a century ago, the trainmaster asked, "What do you want—feather beds?" Since then the term "featherbedding" has been used to describe the purposeful spreading out of work to make jobs.—Ed.] In a recent case on the Minneapolis & St. Louis, for example, a two-unit Diesel locomotive was being prepared to move a freight train. Before the engine left the roundhouse, the mechanical department coupled to it another locomotive unit in which the motor was not operating. The intention was to send the disabled unit on to the next terminal for repairs. The road brakeman that day made exactly the same moves in herding the locomotive from the roundhouse to the train yard as he always did. In this case, however, since the dead unit was attached to the regular train engine, it was necessary for him to walk fifteen additional steps in order to couple the locomotive to the outbound freight train. The brakeman collected an additional day's pay on the ground that moving the dead locomotive unit was switching work not included in his contract. At the same time the railroad was also liable to claim for day's pay from an entire switch crew because of their not being used to move the unit from roundhouse to train yard.

In another recent instance, the M-StL operated a small local passenger train between Albert Lea, Minnesota and Albia, Iowa [a distance of approximately 140 miles]. This was a seven-hour run. If the labor contracts had allowed it, a single crew in each direction could easily have handled these trains over the road between terminals. Crews were changed enroute, however, at an intermediate terminal because it was required by the rules of the Agreement [the National Agreement between railway labor and management under the Railway Labor Act]. This requirement to practically double-crew a comparatively insignificant local passenger train artificially raised the operating cost so that an annual loss of about $29,000 was being sustained. Petition was therefore filed with the Iowa Commerce Commission to discontinue the train because of the operating loss. Our calculations indicated clearly that if a day's work were rendered for a day's pay by the two crews necessary to handle these trains, the operating loss would be almost exactly offset and the train would break even. This was pointed out to the labor organization, but to no avail. Our only alternative was therefore to discontinue the train.

In circumstances such as these, it might be more correct to describe the featherbedding or make-work rules as work-abolishment provisions, since M-StL now has no train, no crew, and no service for passengers on the Albert Lea-Albia route. . . .

A multitude of examples of excess crew requirements might be cited. A case in point is the requirement of a fireman on Diesel freight and yard locomotives. In neither case does the fireman perform any useful service. In stating their case for the fireman on Diesels, the Brotherhood of Locomotive Firemen and Enginemen make much of his alleged value as a safety factor and a "second pair of eyes in the cab." This argument ignores the fact that there are now not two but *three* men on U.S. freight locomotives. Any lookout or safety function of the Diesel fireman therefore duplicates the work of the forward trainman who handles this duty quite adequately since he also rides the locomotive cab. In . . . a recent case a Diesel fireman, with absolutely no other duties to perform than to function as lookout and take action in the event of disability of the engineer, signally failed to perform even that simple duty. Without the slighest effort to avert the impending crash, he allowed the engineer of a Santa Fe passenger train to enter a fifteen mile-per-hour curve in a congested yard area at nearly seventy miles per hour. The train overturned killing 30 passengers and injuring 122 others. Later investigation showed that the engineer had "blacked out" some time before the accident with an epileptic fugue.

The shocking sequel to this tragedy is that when the carrier dismissed the fireman for his gross failure to perform the only function that might conceivably have justified his existence, his union prosecuted the case vigorously through all the channels of appeal. When it finally reached the National Railroad Adjustment Board a Referee, with no railroad experience whatever in his background, ordered him immediately restored to service with

all rights and privileges and with pay for all time lost—some
$14,000. In this fantastic decision, the Referee elected to sub-
stitute his judgment for that of the operating officers responsible
for the safe movement of trains on the Santa Fe. The Referee
concluded that to have expected the fireman to prevent the accident ". . . is to expect too much from any average person. . . ."

In the Diesel era the fireman is an anachronism. He is simply
a hold-over from earlier years when his services were needed on
steam locomotives to generate steam by stoking the fire and
attending to the water level in the boiler. Recognizing this waste
of manpower, the Canadian Pacific Railway . . . notified the
Brotherhood of Locomotive Firemen and Enginemen that with
the transition from steam to Diesel power on the CPR, the
carrier would not use firemen on Diesel freight and switching
locomotives. . . . The carrier offered to continue all firemen in
service with more than three years of seniority regardless of
whether used on steam or Diesel locomotives. Those having less
than three years' service were to be given opportunities for
employment in other branches of the company.

The firemen would thus gradually be eliminated by the forces
of attrition, since no new men were to be hired in the craft.
The labor union flatly rejected this common-sense economy proposal and early in 1957 a nation-wide strike by the Firemen's
Organization tied up the entire railway for nine days during the
dead of winter. After lengthy negotiation, the Canadian government appointed a Royal Commission to explore the question
thoroughly. The Commission, consisting of three eminent jurists,
spent nearly a year riding locomotives and trains in Canada and
in Europe to observe railroad operations at first hand. Their
report supported the carrier's contention that firemen are unnecessary on Diesels and endorsed the railway proposal to
gradually discontinue their use. The union denounced the find-
ings of the Commission and touched off another full scale work
stoppage. . . . The strike failed, however, because an aroused
public opinion came strongly to support of the railway and the
Canadian government. . . .

The magnitude of the "make-work" bill paid annually by
U.S. shippers and travelers who use the rails is shown by a

recent study of just part of it. The price tag on only five major featherbed elements among "operating" unions alone takes over $475 million per year. When only five featherbed elements produce a total of this size, it is evident that the cost of scores of other areas of enforced waste of manpower in the railways is astronomical. [The unions' alleged featherbedding practices are abetted in sixteen states by so-called "full-crew" laws that spell out the required number of brakemen and other crew members to be carried on trains passing through. An Indiana law, for example, requires the use of a third brakeman on freight trains of seventy or more cars. Freight trains from Terre Haute for St. Louis carry this third brakeman for ten miles to the Illinois line. There, since Illinois has no full-crew laws, he is dropped from the train and sent back to Terre Haute by taxi. He collects a full day's pay.—Ed.]

Outlook for the Future

The picture of excess crew rules, make-work practices, and other kinds of featherbedding . . . is essentially a negative one. So negative that unless it is corrected, we can have but little hope for restoring the railroads to vigorous competitive health.

There is, however, an important positive aspect to the railroad labor scene which has tremendous potential if it can be reached and stimulated constructively. This is the huge resource of individual loyalty among railroaders which they have proven many times over. For example, when the M-StL was in dire straits in the 1930's and its larger neighbors were preparing to dismember and gobble it up, rank-and-file employees and union leaders spent thousands of off-duty man-hours and many hard-earned dollars in campaigning for traffic to hold the road together. In more recent years on a national basis, the labor organizations . . . endorsed some of management's proposals to the Smathers Committee such as rate-making freedom, relief from freight and passenger excise taxes, user charges on publicly provided transportation facilities, tighter agricultural exemptions, and several others.

If railway management and its compatriots on the labor side of the table can somehow find the ways and means to work together on these vitally needed changes in labor contracts, a whole new golden age of railroading may open up before us. This is true because there exists a tremendous elasticity of demand for railroad services. It must be remembered that even under their present great handicaps, railroad costs and those of their heavily subsidized competitors are only pennies apart. Inherently, the steel wheel on a steel rail has no peer in efficiency of mass transport. Unshackling of that efficiency through relief from the staggering burden of featherbed costs would permit wholesale revision of railroad rates. With the resulting large increase in traffic volume, many thousands of new job opportunities would be created for railroaders in strong, progressive, tax-paying companies under no shadow of subsidy or threat of public ownership.

Number, Please

To illustrate this point, an interesting parallel may be drawn between railroading and the telephone business. In contrast to the railroad situation, Northwestern Bell Telephone Company, which serves much of M-StL territory, has had almost no opposition from the Communications unions in its fast-moving drive toward mechanization and better operating methods through such devices as dial systems, and the use of microwave to replace costly and vulnerable pole lines. With this freedom to innovate, it has continuously reduced unit costs and has enormously increased the market for its services. For example, in 1925 with "Number Please" operators handling a long distance call Minneapolis to Chicago, it required ten minutes just to put the call through and ring the telephone wanted. Today, with dial equipment the caller in Minneapolis can reach his party in Chicago in only forty-five seconds. With all of the pay increases and inflation that have occurred in the intervening thirty-four years, the amazing thing is that the price of that phone call has been cut from $9.85 in 1925 to only $1.05 today. Looking at this phenomenal performance, a railroad labor leader might ask "Has this meant fewer jobs and lower wages?" Quite the contrary—

the tremendously increased productivity per employee has so expanded the market for telephone service that total employment of telephone operators alone at Northwestern Bell has more than doubled. . . . The average wage has increased more than 450 per cent in the same interval.

Assuming any appreciable reduction in government regulation, if we railroaders could free ourselves from the shackles of archaic labor agreements, we would increase our volume of business just as spectacularly as has Northwestern Bell in the illustration cited above. To the rank-and-file railroader the benefits of doing so would be enormous in terms of higher wages, greater job security, and vastly enlarged horizons for personal development and advancement. The correlative advantages to shippers and passengers, to management people, and to the owners of railroad securities, are too obvious to require cataloging.

Unions in other fields have recognized that steadily increasing productivity is the real key to business growth and true job security. I cannot believe that railroad labor men are any less intelligent.

IT'S NOT FEATHERBEDDING [7]

The railroads are the largest and most important carriers and the most profitable; they realize a margin on gross that is two to three times larger than those of the airlines and truck lines, and is more favorable than that of inland waterway shipping.

Investor confidence in railway securities has been quite strong in recent years; since 1939, railroad stocks have advanced in spectacular fashion. The Dow-Jones average of railroad stocks is more than 400 per cent higher than the average of the pre-World War II year, 1939. Although industrial and utility stocks have also risen dramatically, they have not gone up so far; the Dow-Jones industrial average has increased about 350 per cent over 1939, and the utility average only about 270 per cent over 1939.

The source of the new prosperity of railroad corporations is no secret or mystery; it has resulted directly from the magnificent record of increased efficiency and productivity of railroad em-

[7] From "Railroad Propaganda Ignores Facts." *Economic Trends and Outlook* (monthly publication of AFL-CIO Economic Committee). 4:3-4. S.-O. '59. Reprinted by permission.

ployees during a period in which the benefits and working conditions of railroad employees lagged behind those of other workers. Traffic in 1957 was 75 per cent above what it had been in 1921, but employment and man-hours had almost been cut in half in the period between those two years. Output in traffic units per man-hour increased more than threefold over the years from 1921 to 1957. (Traffic units are a combination of ton-miles and passenger miles; they are used by the Interstate Commerce Commission, the Bureau of Labor Statistics, and by both the carriers and the employees to measure railroad output.)

In general, railway productivity has improved more than productivity in other industries. Comparisons of man-hour output of the Bureau of Labor Statistics are available for railroads and manufacturing industries. For the period from 1939 to 1956, railroad productivity increased by 92.9 per cent while manufacturing productivity increased by 48.8 per cent. The increase on the railroads was just about twice the increase in other industries. In service industries, such as the railways, employee performance is a very important factor in improving output.

During the last decade, railroad wages and working conditions have twice been held in check by long term agreements— from 1951 to 1953 and from 1956 to 1959. As a result, no changes were made in those years in many benefits and working conditions such as vacations, holidays, and insurance. . . .

The progressive increases in employee productivity through the years have produced corresponding increases in the revenue yield per employee. Even since the end of the war, revenues per employee have doubled—from $5,612 in 1946 to $11,379 in 1958. In the same postwar years revenues per dollar of compensation have also increased modestly—from $1,829 in 1946 to $1,940 in 1958.

Are Railroad Workers "Featherbedding"?

In view of the sensational efficiency and productivity record of railroad workers, the corporation claim that they are "featherbedding" is preposterous. Such a performance could not be accomplished by a work force that was being paid for doing no work, or for doing too little work for the pay it has received. If railroad workers are "featherbedding," it would show in the record of their efficiency and output per man-hour. But railroad propagandists continue to repeat incessantly the slogans about "firemen who tend no fires and brakemen who handle no brakes," and about the "antiquated pay system that applies to all employees in road operating service."

Actually, very few firemen were "tending fires" on American railroads in the later years of the steam era. Most steam locomotives had automatic coal stokers, or were oil burning. But firemen, in both steam locomotives and Diesel locomotives, have had very important duties and they still do:

1. They are in charge of the power plant, to see that it functions efficiently and continuously in response to the engineer's operation of controls. When multiple unit Diesel locomotives first came into use, many railroads used two firemen, or a fireman and a mechanic, so as to insure complete monitoring of all units. (Diesel locomotives are frequently linked together and operated by one set of controls. When steam locomotives were linked in "double headers," it was necessary to have one crew for each locomotive.) Today, generally, one fireman does the whole job.

2. The fireman must maintain a constant watch on his side of the train while the engineer maintains a similar watch on the opposite side. These trains today are long, heavy, fast, and very valuable; they become instruments of destruction if not carefully controlled. The fireman and engineer both must maintain constant watch on the track ahead, on the signals, and on possible highway traffic at grade crossings.

3. The fireman is an assistant to the engineer, and a relief engineer available to take over in an emergency, should anything happen to the engineer.

The suggestion that brakemen handle no brakes is equally absurd. Consider the following statement in an article which appeared recently:

> In sixteen states, laws spell out the required number of brakemen and other crew members to be carried on trains passing through. Many of these laws go back fifty years, to a time when railroad cars required hand-braking. Today, trains are equipped with power brakes, but the old laws remain on the books.

This statement implies—without directly stating—that brakemen no longer use hand brakes. Consider the following statistics reported by the Interstate Commerce Commission: In the first six months of 1959, one train service employee was killed and 227 were injured operating hand brakes. In the five years, 1954 to 1958, 21 men were killed and 3,286 were injured operating hand brakes. The statement or suggestion that brakemen do not handle brakes is a typical railroad propaganda misrepresentation.

The minimum train crew in road freight service is only five men—an engineer, a fireman, a conductor, and two brakemen. In some instances, because of an excessive number of cars in the train, or the character of the work performed en route, an additional brakeman is added. This has been the standard minimum crew for over forty years, and it hasn't increased in size in spite of the fact that trains today are longer, heavier, faster, and potentially more destructive than ever before. State governments, and railway unions, seeking to protect the public as well as railway workers, knew that safety of operations required the employment of this minimum work force of five men when the laws or rules were adopted. Statistics of the Interstate Commerce Commission prove that the minimum crew is even more necessary today than it was back in the days of steam power.

In the mid-nineteen thirties, when most trains were pulled by steam power, the accident rate per million miles on American railways was 5.76. From 1951 to 1956 the comparable average rate was 7.24—26 per cent higher than during the steam power period. This is obviously no time for the government or the employees to lower the safety standards in railway operation.

The Operating Employees' Pay System

The pay system by which road operating employees are compensated is a piece rate system where the unit of pay is the mile run. Incentive systems need to be brought up-to-date occasionally with the passage of time and changes in conditions. Through the years some changes have been made in the so-called dual pay system, but some additional overhauling and improvement is still needed.

The question arises, however: in which direction is the wage system obsolete? In general it may be said that the existing system is completely unfair now to the employees.

Among the many elements in the system that are out-of-line with current industrial practices is the overtime basis. Most American workers today have a five-day, forty-hour week with premium overtime after eight hours a day and forty hours a week, as well as for work on rest-days and on holidays. Road operating employees have no fixed basis for premium overtime—their overtime base varies with the speed of operations. They may be— they frequently are—required to work up to ten, twelve, fourteen or even more hours in a day at straight time.

Furthermore, many of them work seven days per week with no Sundays off, no holidays off, and only straight time pay when they work on such days.

Yes, these conditions are obsolete, and the employees hope to bring them up to current standards in future bargaining. These elements certainly are forty years behind the times, but they are not mentioned in the sweeping attacks on employees in railroad corporation propaganda. The intent of this company campaign is to create a climate in which they may add new injustices to the present system without correcting the real inequities the employees are now suffering from.

On November 1, 1959, the wage and rules' agreements of all railway employees became open for change. Practically all railway unions requested wage increases and improvements in such employee benefits as vacations, holidays and health and welfare protection.

The railway corporations themselves served notice on all classes of workers for wage cuts and reductions in other conditions of work. The American public has a heavy interest in seeing that the . . . negotiations are handled through the orderly procedures of the Railway Labor Act and not by misleading propaganda, and that they yield settlements that are fair to both the employees and the companies. [For a description of these procedures see "Railroad Labor and Labor Relations," in this section, above.] Railway workers are not asking for the moon. They seek only those improvements that other workers have been getting during the three years their agreements have been frozen. They will fight for fair treatment if necessary, but they hope that the companies will not prevent a fair fight.

RAILROADS FOR WAR [8]

Warfare goes on in all seasons and all weathers, and no one can say with certainty where we may be called upon to defend our national security. Planning for such an emergency must take account of logistical problems imposed by this wide range of climatic and topographical possibilities. . . . [and] all military logistical planning is built around the railroad as the primary reliance, with other transport as important but auxiliary and supplemental carriers.

Railroads can go anywhere that a railway can be laid, and experience has shown that a railway can be laid in most places where it is needed. We have used railroads in the deserts of North Africa, the tundra and permafrost of Alaska, the mountains of Korea, and the plains of northern France and Germany. They have operated dependably in temperatures of 30 degrees or more below zero in Alaska, Canada, and our own northern states, and likewise in the blazing heat of Iran. With their variety of cars and their firm roadbed, they can and do handle every kind, size, and weight of shipments. They keep going in all kinds of storms and bad weather, and all conditions of visibility; it is the infrequent exception to a general rule when rail transport is not the last to give up and stop.

No other type of transport has nearly so large a share of these attributes of versatility and dependability. Water carriers can go only where there are streams or other bodies of water of sufficient depth to provide navigable channels. These channels must be clear of underwater hazards to navigation. When they freeze up in winter navigation stops, unless costly and troublesome ice-breaker service is available. Fast loading and unloading of vessels are problems still not entirely solved.

[8] From *Rail Transport and the Winning of Wars*, by General James A. Van Fleet, United States Army (Ret.), Commanding General of the Eighth Army in Korea, 1951-1953. Association of American Railroads. Transportation Building. Washington 6, D.C. 1956. p. 63-71. Reprinted by permission of the author.

Highway transport is indispensable for beach and port clearance during and immediately after landing in enemy-held territory. It also has a firm place in supply of fast-moving forces beyond railheads, as in the famous XYZ motor transport operation which supported our advance beyond the Rhine in . . . early 1945, [but] highway transport for volume operation is scarcely less limited than railroads by need for a roadway over which to operate. Its relatively small units are correspondingly limited as to size and weight of loads which can be carried. It is prodigal of manpower and fuel in relation to load transported. It is more susceptible than rail transport to interruption from adverse weather, visibility, and roadway conditions. Also of some importance, highway transport lacks the long tradition of make-do and self-reliance so well established on railroads. It likewise lacks the standardization of facilities and methods, the communications systems and other elements of disciplined, controlled traffic movement, and the close-knit national organization which characterize railroads and are so valuable to national security.

Pipelines are tremendously efficient and valuable in their own field, but this field is strictly limited to a few special commodities. Except for their pumping facilities, they have little vulnerability to enemy attack. On the other hand, they are not readily provided in large capacity where they do not already exist. They will always have their own place in the logistical picture, but it can never be a primary place.

Air transport also is tremendously valuable in its place, but again this will not, in all probability, be a primary place. For emergency movements where great speed is the essential factor it has no equal. On the other hand, it can be used for sustained volume movements (such as the Berlin Air Lift only at extremely high cost in plane deterioration as well as in manpower and fuel. The planes themselves are not well adapted for easy loading and unloading, especially of heavy freight. Load per vehicle is low in relation to fuel and power demand and crew time. Weather conditions often are a limiting factor (as during the Battle of the Bulge, in December 1944, for example). Air transport also is affected by extent and activity of enemy air power, whereas we found in Korea that absolute air supremacy did not enable us to shut off enemy supply by rail.

Considering all these factors, and in the light of technological developments in sight or "in the works," no form or combination of forms of transport appears likely to challenge the key place of railroads in the military logistical picture. The combat commander of tomorrow will use and value all kinds of transport in their respective fields, and current military training is along this line. But it also is now, and in my judgment will continue for many years to be, standard training doctrine that in military logistics the railroad is basic. . . .

[More than 97 per cent of all troops, more than 90 per cent of all Army equipment and supplies and about 90 per cent of all Navy equipment and supplies were transported by rail during World War II. With one fourth fewer employees, one third fewer locomotives, one fourth fewer freight cars and one third fewer passenger cars than in World War I, the railroads of the United States, each month on the average, moved about twice as many troops, performed more than twice as many passenger-miles of service, moved more than five times as much Army freight and express, twenty times as much Navy freight for overseas destinations, and nearly double as many ton-miles of freight of all kinds as they moved in World War I—and they performed this unprecedented task without the prolonged delays and the congestion of the First World War.

Federal operation of the railroads and allied agencies during and following the First World War (from January 1, 1918, to March 1, 1920, and including the guaranty period ending August 31, 1920) cost the American taxpayers $1.641 billion, or an average of nearly $2 million a day, notwithstanding increases in freight rates and passenger fares during the period of Federal control. In World War II, ending in August 1945, the railroads were privately operated at no loss whatever to the taxpayers or the Federal Government; instead, during the war period 1942-1945 they paid an average of $3.172 million a day in Federal income taxes.

When the losses under Federal control in the First World War and taxes paid in both wars are taken into account, it is found that the Federal Government was more than $5 million a day better off under private operation in World War II than under government operation in World War I. Moreover, freight rates remained at approximately prewar levels throughout World War II, and passenger fares advanced but slightly.

From December 1941 to August 1945, inclusive, a total of 113,891 special troop trains were operated for distances ranging all the way up to three thousand miles or more. In addition, the railroads handled an even greater number of special troop cars in regular trains. The special train movements involved 303,003 coach trips, 511,385 sleeping car trips, 142,706 baggage and kitchen car trips, and 193,784 refrigerator, box, flat, and gondola car trips, besides an almost equal movement of empty cars to and from loading and unloading points.

From December 1, 1941, to the end of August 1945, the railroads transported approximately 43.7 million members of the United States Army, Navy, Marines, and Coast Guard in special troop or hospital trains, or in special cars attached to regular trains. The average monthly movement during this forty-five-month period was 971,110 troops. This was more than twice the average monthly movement during World War I.]

The specific amount that may be carried by rail in any future war is difficult to predict, due to many variables associated with atomic war. One quantitative estimate made by the Office of Defense Mobilization, covering an assumed three-year mobilization period, indicates that there will be little change in the basic distribution among the various types of carriers of all domestic traffic. However, due to continued industrial expansion and the increase of population, ton-miles of freight traffic handled by the railroads will be 25 to 30 per cent in excess of the peak load of World War II. And even heavier requirements could result from lengthened hauls necessitated by alternate routings to by-pass damaged areas. This estimate includes all domestic freight, civilian and military.

It is therefore only logical to conclude that in the event of a third global conflict, railroads will be called upon to move the bulk of our military traffic as they have in the past. The railroads remain the single mode of transport capable of meeting the greatest part of the military traffic requirements.

Why Railroads Are Indispensable

Our recent wars in Europe and in Korea were fought over large land areas (in contrast with our island war against Japan). Logistical lessons of these land wars clearly demonstrate the indispensability of rail transport. Only railroads can provide and maintain the volume of transportation, day after day, required by large modern armies, highly mechanized and with great firepower.

Experience as a combat commander forcefully impressed me with the ability of railroads to deliver large quantities of supplies with dependable regularity in face of continual enemy efforts at interdiction and interruption. I saw these characteristics in evidence both on our own railroads and on those supplying the enemy. Therefore, I know them to be inherent in the railroad itself and not peculiar to our own skill and ingenuity—though the performance of our own railroad personnel was superlative. . . .

We had skilled personnel to operate our military railroads from the ports to the front lines in World War II and Korea because we were able to draw upon railway organizations of the United States for trained personnel and unlimited know-how. In World War II railroads supplied more than forty thousand skilled railroad men, including some of their top executives, for the Military Railway Service, which operated railroads on various fighting fronts. These forces were, of course, in addition to hundreds of thousands of railway employees inducted into other branches of military service. In Korea, too, we drew extensively upon railroads of the United States for experienced leadership and know-how in railway operations. In case of another war, need for skilled railway men may be even greater than in the last. . . .

The lesson of this experience is plain. The railroads of the United States are a great basic military asset. They are as much

a part of the military strength of the nation as our Army, Navy,
Air Force, and Marines, because none of these great armed
services could long operate without the logistical support which
railroads provide. No other form of transport, nor all other
forms combined, could take over the job of railroads, because
they all lack some of the inherent characteristics on which the
military value of railroads is based.

This is almost certainly going to be true in any future defense
emergency, as it has always been true in the past ever since railroads became a military factor. If our future military activities
are beyond our own shores, railroads of the United States will
play the same vital part as in World Wars I and II, and the
Korean war. They will support and make possible the national
productive effort on the huge scale required to carry on modern
warfare. They will provide the high-volume, long-haul, dependable transport to get the men and the tools of war to training
camps and ports as needed. They will supply trained men and
officers for our military railway units. And they will be called
upon to handle the great bulk of the civilian passenger travel of
all kinds that is an inevitable part of a military effort. . . .

In the event of another war, transportation facilities un-
doubtedly would be attacked. However, as was demonstrated in
Korea, in Italy, in France, in Germany, and in England, enemy
attacks would find more vulnerable and more profitable targets in
the sources of raw materials, the points of manufacture, and the
bases from which our counter-offensive would be launched, than
they would in attempts to knock out routes of transportation.
And, as experience in all these countries showed, of all forms of
transportation none is more difficult to knock out, nor more re-
sistant to enemy attack, than railroads. No form of transportation has such powers of recuperation, or draws so lightly upon
reserves of materials and manpower, as railroads.

In any future national defense emergency, as in all past military efforts since railroads came into being, we shall without
doubt have imperative need for the quantity and type of transport
which only railroads can supply. Therefore, we have now and
always will have vital need for strong, vigorous, progressive rail-

roads, with reserves of traffic capacity and trained manpower upon which the armed forces can draw for their own combat and strategic requirements. To maintain such a rail plant in readiness, it must be used in peacetime.

FOUR SYSTEMS FOR THE FUTURE [9]

It is still not too late for U.S. railroads to do what they should have done years ago: consolidate into three or four noncompetitive, integrated, regional systems that would . . . eliminate thousands of miles of duplicate track, close down hundreds of redundant yards and terminals, let the roads move traffic more expeditiously and cheaply, and save hundreds of millions of dollars a year. In fact, large-scale consolidation is probably the only measure that will enable the railroad industry to make enough money to survive as private enterprise. . . .

There are a few hopeful signs. The Great Northern and Northern Pacific want to combine with the Burlington to form an 18,000-mile system. The Erie, Lackawanna, and Delaware & Hudson are exploring the idea of forming a great new system in the East. A recent plan to merge the Chicago & North Western and the Milwaukee is dormant, but not dead. The New York Central and the Pennsylvania, which together do nearly a fifth of the country's railroad business, are studying a consolidation that could shake the transportation world. While these proposed consolidations may not yet be too late, they are too few.

However, they have one good thing in common: for the first time in more than fifty years, they aim to unite so-called competing roads. The existence of hundreds of separate railroad companies is usually justified by the assumption, long outdated, that most of them compete with one another. Compete in price they certainly do not: exempt from the antitrust laws, they get together and set prices under supervision of the ICC. Although they talk of "service competition," the service they render suffers as much as it gains from this kind of competition. Just as the high-cost railroads in effect set the price levels, so the lame and

[9] From "A Plan to Save the Railroads," by Gilbert Burck, member of the Board of Editors of *Fortune* magazine. *Fortune.* 58:82-6+. Reprinted by special permission from the August 1958 issue of *Fortune* magazine. © 1958 by Time Inc.

the halt lines tend to set the service standards. Railroad rivalry is actually the rivalry of cartel members who go through the motions of competition, with the result that costs are much greater than they would be if the railroads did not pretend to compete at all.

A sound economic reason no longer exists, in any case, to compel U.S. railroads to compete with one another. Their multiplicity is technologically and functionally obsolete, a relic of a past when the rails served local needs and had no rivals. Traffic today flows in regional and national rather than in the old parochial patterns. Most loaded freight cars move over two or more railroads between their origin and their destination; whether railroads wanted to or not, they have had to function more and more as parts of a national system, but without obtaining the advantages of being units in a single system. Moreover, they face real competition from the enterprising highway, waterway, and air carriers. They will not be able to meet this competition without cutting out the wastes of inter-railroad rivalry. . . .

Too Much Plant

Now let us see how consolidation might save the railroads as much as $1 billion a year. To begin with, so long as the industry is set up as 634 separate companies, it is forced to maintain far too much plant—tracks, terminals, shops, buildings, and freight cars—for the work it does. Any railroad, of course, must maintain sufficient excess capacity to accommodate traffic peaks, some expansion, and national emergencies. But "competition" among the roads has always forced them to maintain vastly more capacity than they needed; and technological advances now enable them to handle so much more traffic with so much less trackage and other facilities that they can accommodate any immediately foreseeable increase in traffic with considerably less plant than they now maintain.

Like U.S. farmers, U.S. railroads are a problem partly because they can produce more and more with less and less. Twenty-five years ago, for instance, freight trains of some large eastern roads moved as many as 150,000 tons of freight a day over four-track main lines. Today, with electronic signal controls and other improvements as well as more powerful locomotives, heavier and faster trains can roll twice as much tonnage over the same track. . . . Ten years from now, even heavier and faster trains will be able to move half again as much tonnage over the same track.

Thus the railroads can effect enormous savings—and improve service, too—by eliminating duplicate lines. A good example of how this can be done is the Erie-Lackawanna coordination now under way in New York State. For seventy-seven miles, in the valleys of the Susquehanna and Chemung rivers, the Erie and Lackawanna main lines parallel each other closely. Together they have been handling an average of a few more than sixty trains every twenty-four hours—not enough, these days, to begin to tax the capacity of either line. In . . . [1955] the two companies worked out a coordination scheme. Trains will be run over what was the Erie main line; yards and stations will be maintained jointly. Fifty-four miles of double and eighteen miles of single track will be abandoned. A yard will also be eliminated at Elmira, leaving forty acres available for industrial development. Yet freight schedules will be accelerated, and industries along the line will be served better than before. The improvement will require $1.6 million worth of new signaling, interlocking, and track connections. But the roads estimate that the change will save no less than $1.09 million annually—$800,000 in maintenance, $160,000 net in switching and locomotive expenses, and $130,000 in station expenses—a 68 per cent annual return on the new investment.

Throughout the country there may be more than thirty thousand miles of line that could be coordinated in this way. But so long as all railroads are separate companies, each with its own strategy, and reluctant to share some hard-won or inherited advantage with a rival, deals like the Erie-Lackawanna are hard to make. Let the roads be consolidated, however, and a larger strategy automatically dominates policy. The consolidation of duplicate trackage then presents few more difficulites than combining two adjacent grocery stores. [In the spring of 1960, when this book went to press, it was expected that the ICC would soon approve a proposed corporate merger of the Erie and Lackawanna Railroads.—Ed.]

Consolidation, furthermore, would allow the railroads to concentrate traffic on their most economic routes—that is, routes demanding the least in energy and repairs. The inherent economy of a route is determined by curves and grades, chiefly the latter. It takes twice as much energy to roll a train slowly up a grade rising only three feet in a thousand (.3 per cent) as it does to run the same train at high speed on level track; and it takes six times as much energy to move a train slowly up a 1 per cent grade as to move it fast over level track. Thus the "out-of-pocket" costs (wages, fuel, locomotive maintenance, maintenance-of-way expenses affected by use) of hauling a thousand gross tons a mile come to between $1.25 and $1.30 over a fairly level and straight "division," but to more than $1.50 over a division with frequent grades of over .5 per cent.

Unfortunately, few railroads have really analyzed their line costs in detail. But the measurements that do exist suggest that much freight is being hauled over routes whose out-of-pocket costs may be 15 per cent higher than on an alternate route or combination of routes. In almost any business but the railroad industry, with its cartelized rate structure, this could be a ruinous difference for the company with the higher costs. . . .

Consolidation would not only mean using the most economic track; it would also eliminate or greatly reduce the practice of dispatching loaded freight cars over roundabout routes. According to ICC studies, the average loaded car rolls some 13 per cent farther than the shortest route between its origin and destination. Students of transportation conservatively estimate that this "circuity" now costs the railroads more than $100 million a year.

Some of the circuity, of course, is a byproduct of the railroads' service to shippers who want to unload or load part of their cargo at points en route; but most of it occurs because the company that solicits the traffic rolls that traffic as far it can over its own rails. . . .

A vast amount of time and legal talent is devoted to comput-
ing, checking, and litigating the division of freight revenues.
The road originating a cargo usually gets a premium, and the
road hauling it, say 250 miles, usually gets more than the road
hauling it 150 miles. But the precise division of the total charge
is full of complexities. Fantastically, a company that can prove
its costs are *higher* than the costs of connecting roads can usually
wangle a larger share of the total, if a disputed revenue-division
case goes to the ICC, than it otherwise could. Consolidation
would all but end this vexatious problem.

Sending "Foreigners" Home

U.S. railroads operate nearly two million freight cars. Under
consolidation, fewer than 1.5 million cars would suffice for all
needs, including national emergencies. The main reason railroads
need so many cars now is that they haul too many of them around
empty—at a waste of some $200 million a year.

Each company buys and retains title to its own cars; each pays
. . . [$2.88] a day rental for every "foreign" car in use on its
line. [See "The Long Voyage Home" in this section, above.]
This per diem is cheap enough; indeed, it does not bring the
owner a fair return. But when business is slack and cars are
plentiful, no railroad likes to keep foreign cars on its line at . . .
[$2.88] a day per car. Instead of keeping them until they can be
loaded nearby, it promptly shoots them homeward. (Or if it
needs some foreign cars but has a surplus of them, it returns the
old, beat-up ones and keeps the new.) And so empty cars are
hauled back and forth at just the time railroads can least afford
the unnecessary expense.

On the other hand, when business is brisk and cars are scarce,
a company naturally hangs on to all the cars it can get, even if
the owners need the cars worse. Consequently, railroads originating a lot of traffic have to maintain an inordinately large supply
of cars, keeping many in reserve.

Whether business is brisk or bad, railroads understandably
bother to repair foreign cars only if absolutely necessary even
though they are compensated by the owners. And since the

average freight car spends most of its time on foreign lines, car owners neither build nor maintain their cars as well as they should; nor do they retire them promptly when their economic life has ended. Why build and maintain your rolling stock to high standards when the other guy gets the most use out of it?

Here again regional consolidation would almost automatically introduce higher standards in car design, construction, and maintenance, and would also end today's senseless system of oversupply and maldistribution.

Put the Terminals Together

Terminal costs, the scourge of all modern transportation, are especially burdensome for railroads. No less than a third of their money and two thirds of their operating time are spent on terminals—freight and passenger stations, "classification" yards, and other facilities devoted to combining cars into trains or breaking up trains into cars.

Although the carriers have recently managed to reduce terminal costs, here again they are restrained from achieving genuine economy by the individual road's reluctance to share an advantageous facility with a competitor. Except for the yards of jointly owned switching and terminal companies, the railroads operate few yards together. Consequently, a freight car moving from road A to road B usually must first be "classified" or switched in A's yard, wait to be moved to B's yard by a transfer engine, and then be switched in B's yard. This triple play may take several days, and it adds more than $30 to the cost of each interline car movement.

Simply by making it possible for heavier trains to be run farther without being broken up, consolidation would reduce the proportion of cars requiring yard handling. More important, consolidation would generate huge direct savings in terminal costs. In one merger now under discussion, for example, the largest time and money saver would be a joint yard that none of the participating railroads could justify alone. The proposed yard would cut terminal costs nearly 50 per cent by eliminating three old yards and intermediate transfer movements. It would also save up to twelve hours on through car movements.

Other economies of consolidation are fairly obvious. Last year railroads spent some $1.8 billion on fuel, materials, and supplies. Much of their purchasing is based on reciprocity: you ship on my road and I'll buy your product. When there are no competing roads to ship on, reciprocity should be heavily reduced. Together with mass buying, this could make for sizable savings. Some optimists have estimated the savings at 10 per cent of present purchases, but even 5 per cent of $1.8 billion works out to $90 million, or close to a quarter of the carriers' dividend payments in 1957.

The $700 Million Problem

Consolidation should end the carriers' shiftless attitude toward their passenger business, which is losing them $700 million a year, a sum nearly equal to the average net income of the whole industry in the best postwar years. For consolidation would enable the roads, without any loss of prestige, to eliminate duplicate runs and unprofitable trains, and concentrate on the most expeditious and remunerative routes. If, as some students of transportation believe, the carriers can still make money on passenger traffic by developing a true mass transportation service, a consolidated system can do it efficiently.

Finally, there is money to be saved in reorganizing less-than-carload freight service and establishing centralized equipment-repair shops. Analyses made in 1934-35 by the Federal Co-ordinator of Transportation indicated that these two areas, at that time, could yield economies totaling more than $500 million a year. Railroads have since improved their performance in both departments, but not nearly enough.

All the economies described above add up to at least $1 billion a year: $400 million in terminal costs, about $100 million now spent on maintenance and operation of unnecessary line, at least $300 million through improved car routing and utilization, $75 million or more in purchasing, and perhaps several hundred millions by centralizing equipment-repair shops and reorganizing less-than-carload service.

Several consolidation plans were advanced during the 1930's and the estimates of potential savings then ranged from 15 to 30 per cent of operating expenses. Most students of consolidation today agree that regional mergers could save at least 12 per cent of current operating costs, or around $1 billion a year.

But there is much more to consolidation than saving money— for the country as well as the roads. Only consolidation can enable the carriers to achieve their great efficiency potential. With the present number of competing lines, even the largest railroads usually don't have enough traffic to operate heavy, long-distance trains between their terminals at sufficiently frequent intervals to maintain good service. . . .

Consolidation would also enable railroads to revise their rate structure, which is even more obsolete than their pretensions to competition. . . . [See "Freight Wars and Freight Rates" in this section, above.] Gradually it would erect a rate structure bearing a rational and consistent relationship to the cost of providing the service and thus immeasurably strengthen the railroads' competitive position vis-à-vis the truckers.

The Great Consolidators

There is nothing new or untried about consolidation. The early railroads, which produced mostly "retail" or local carload transportation, had to consolidate as the need arose for trainload or mass transportation over longer distances. Later, the great railroad monopolists like Vanderbilt, Huntington, Hill, Morgan, and Harriman initiated a nation-wide wave of consolidation that reached its peak between 1890 and 1900. Whatever their motives, the monopolists had economics on their side.

But then the movement began to slow down. One reason for the slowdown was the depression of 1907, which threw several great roads into bankruptcy. Another reason was the Sherman Antitrust Act, which the Department of Justice employed to dissolve the Hill system (in 1904) and the Harriman system (in 1913). Another reason was the government's own "consolidation program," as written into the Transportation Act of 1920, which did anything but promote consolidation.

Rarely if ever has any Congress enacted legislation so self-contradictory as the act of 1920. The ICC was directed to prepare a consolidation plan. Congress recognized that price competition between the roads was impractical if not impossible; yet it specified that after consolidation, competition must be maintained wherever possible. It also specified that existing routes and trade channels must be maintained wherever practicable, and that the consolidated systems must earn substantially the same rate of return under uniform rates. Things must change, in other words, but nothing must change. The carriers must compete, yet they must not compete.

The ICC struggled with this fantastic mandate for the best part of a decade. It prepared a preliminary plan in 1921, and for years listened to the protests of railroads, shippers, municipalities, and labor. A final plan, delivered to the world shortly after the Wall Street crash in 1929, proposed to consolidate the nation's railroads into twenty-one competing systems. But the ICC had no power to enforce the plan, and railroads simply let the matter drop. Meantime, except for a few scattered attempts at mergers, notably those of the Van Sweringen brothers of Cleveland, who tried to consolidate the Erie, Chesapeake & Ohio, Nickel Plate, and Missouri Pacific, consolidation languished.

Of the several new consolidation plans advanced during the depressed 1930's, the most seriously regarded was the Prince Plan, drawn up in 1933 by John W. Barriger and named for its sponsor, the effervescent industrialist-financier, Frederick Prince. Necessarily hewing to the terms of the 1920 law, the Prince Plan preserved existing trade routes and competition at main points. But it cut out much wasteful competition by dividing the carriers into seven regional systems. On the sound premise that the nation was supporting too many high-cost, light-traffic lines, the plan suggested radical line mergers and a scaling down of railroad properties as a prelude to intensive development of the main routes.

Barriger estimated the plan's eventual savings at 25 per cent of operating expenses, or $743 million (equivalent to $2.3 billion today)—though a deliberately critical study estimated the plan's savings at considerably less. In retrospect, two things can be said of the Prince Plan: (1) it did not go far enough, and (2) if the nation had adopted it, a modern, prosperous railroad system would today be providing better rail transportation at lower prices.

In the Transportation Act of 1940, Congress ignored the ICC plan of 1929 without providing for another plan. The 1940 act says only that consolidation is lawful if consistent with the public interest, and that the ICC, in judging consolidation, shall give weight to such considerations as adequate service to the public, compensation to labor, etc. Nothing is said about preserving competition and existing trade routes.

Why didn't the railroads rush in to take advantage of the change? During the war, of course, they were too busy moving a colossal volume of freight and passengers. And their burst of postwar prosperity, brief and meager though it was, presumably lulled them into inactivity. Only belatedly have a few competing lines begun to work on regional consolidation projects.

Theoretically, there should be as few systems as possible, and one big system for the whole country would be best of all. Only a single system could wholly eliminate duplicate track and terminals, end circuitous routing, and rationally concentrate traffic. But a single national system probably would be regarded by most railroaders as too radical and also too hard to manage, and might arouse insurmountable political opposition. And a single system might also seem too easy for the government to take over—though it is not the size of a railroad system but its inability to make money under private operation that will force it into government ownership. In any event, a single system would have to be split into regional operating units.

A Four-System Network

A truly national rail network could logically be divided into four large systems [a Northeastern system and a Southern system east of the Mississippi; a Northwestern and Southwestern system west of the Mississippi]. Of the four, the Northeastern would be the largest, with more than 400,000 employees, 59,000 miles of line, and gross revenues of $5 billion.

But how, the practical railroad man will ask, do you propose to manage a system encompassing as much as 59,000 miles of line and employing several hundred thousand people? The large railroad is a transportation factory located everywhere and yet in no one place.

Existing railroads as large and complex as the Pennsylvania and New York Central have not yet solved the rather elementary problem of how to decentralize and yet enable top management to keep in touch with daily operations without devoting most of its time to them. By their very nature, railroads are run like armies at war: operations come first. Officials with the important and satisfying jobs are primarily line officers; a purely staff officer, even at the highest level, is like a general cooling his heels in the Pentagon while the battle is raging two thousand miles away. Every good railroad president spends a large part of his time in his business car, getting the feel of what is happening on the road.

Management of a large consolidated system might well be set up like this: (1) line responsibilities would be decentralized under district vice presidents possessing large autonomy (they could be called presidents if that would help); (2) central staff officers without line responsibilities would have authority over system functions like rate making, personnel policies, purchasing, big engineering jobs, and locomotive and car distribution; (3) a large, high-caliber engineering staff under a vice president would be assigned the critical job of analyzing the system and constantly looking for ways of making it more efficient; and (4) a system of communications would enable top officials to keep in constant touch with the front line without spending most of their time on it.

This is not impossible. The probability, indeed, is that a drastic consolidation, because it would break sharply with the past, would help solve the management problems that plague the railroads today, rather than create insoluble new ones.

The Roadblocks

How could regional consolidation be taken out of the realm of theory and made a reality under today's conditions? Looking for the answer, one speculates on what a man like Edward Harriman, who sixty years ago aimed to control nearly all U.S. railroads worth owning, might do if he were alive today.

At [1958] market prices—$12 a share for Pennsylvania stock and $16 for New York Central—a latter-day Harriman could acquire 38 per cent control of these lines, which only a few years ago managed to earn more than $100 million between them, for as little as $100 million. Consolidating and improving these great properties as the original Harriman did with the Union Pacific and Central Pacific sixty years ago, he could in a few years convert them into a huge money-maker, earning upwards of $200 million and paying dividends of $100 million or more. Stock . . . worth $14 a share [in 1958] might then be worth more than $100 a share.

Indeed, a man as audacious and resourceful as Harriman, given great financial backing, could conceivably get control of most of the important railroads and thus force the rest to join him. Employing imaginative, farsighted managers, he could convert the railroads into everything they should be: efficient, progressive, national in scope, profitable—and indispensable.

He could—if there weren't so many obstacles in the way of consolidation today that even a super-Harriman would be put off by them. As the Van Sweringen brothers discovered twenty-five years ago, the merging process is complex, time-consuming, frustrating, and man-killing. And although the Interstate Commerce Commission is no longer dedicated to preserving existing channels of trade or inter-railroad competition, there are still plenty of other obstacles to consolidation. Unless a consolidator could get firm control over the prosperous carriers, they would naturally be unenthusiastic about merging with any other road, strong or weak. Many rail executives, of course, would fear loss of prestige and security under consolidation, and they would have to be won over. And the owners of the roads' securities would have to be persuaded to agree on the terms. The bondholders would presumably make no trouble; but the minority common stockholders, even after a merger had been approved by the majority, could bring suit against the deal. The wrangling could take years.

Consolidation proposals must be argued before the ICC, which has been catering to special interests so long it has almost forgotten there is such a thing as the national interest. The ICC must give ear to communities that hate to lose railroad property taxes when a line is scaled down, to shippers who fear that service may be impaired, to truck lines that fear railroad competition—and particularly to labor, which could be counted on to wage effective war against consolidation because most of its economies would be realized as reduced labor costs. As long ago as 1936, railroad labor forced Congress to write into the law the so-called "Washington Agreement," which provides that workers displaced by consolidation must be compensated for as long as five years.

And there is also Congress itself. Although few if any professional railroad-baiters are left in Congress, it is hard to imagine any Congressman figuring there were many votes in a crusade for consolidation.

[A ten-year plan to improve the U.S. transportation picture was submitted to the President in March 1960 by the Department of Commerce and transmitted by the President to Congress. The following are the major provisions of the plan: (1) repeal of the 10 per cent Federal tax on passenger travel; (2) higher fees and some new fees to be collected from users of federally financed facilities such as airways and waterways; (3) less governmental regulation of rail, trucking, and air rates; (4) encouragement of rail mergers that increase efficiency. Congress, facing the 1960 elections, failed to take any action on the proposals but they are expected to be resubmitted at a later session.—Ed.]

Unless all railroads were engaged in consolidation at the same time, moreover, some of the most persuasive and serious objections to it would come from lines whose managers and stockholders could reasonably complain that other mergers were putting them at a disadvantage. If strong railroads, for example, were to merge with other strong railroads and leave the weaker lines scattered around to fend for themselves, the ICC could interpret the law to give sympathetic (and plausible) heed to the weaklings' cries for succor.

To overcome these numerous obstacles, inside and outside Washington, the government must take some initiative. The truth is that any industry as far gone in government regulation as the railroad industry can be manumitted only through the good offices of government. One suggestion, made by a rail official who favors consolidation but argues that it would take the ICC twenty-five years to prepare a plan, is that Congress simply adopt a resolution to the effect (1) that large-scale consolidation is consistent with the public interest, (2) that the railroads be urged to undertake consolidations, and (3) that the ICC both render staff assistance to railroads studying consolidation and give applications for consolidation a high priority. . . .

Needed: A Push

The consolidation projects now under way, assuming they are given sympathetic attention by the ICC, might in time be successfully consummated. Suppose, however, that Congress were to expedite them. Suppose it were to declare large-scale consolidation in the public interest, and instruct the ICC to give aid and priority to consolidation projects. And suppose Congress were also to give the carriers two years or so to develop their own plans, postponing meantime the establishment of a government consolidation authority.

Thus stimulated, the roads' current consolidation projects could start a wave of mergers that might take in most of the lines in the country. The Great Northern-Northern Pacific-Burlington combination [the James J. Hill roads] would probably force the Chicago & North Western and Milwaukee roads to revive their merger scheme and combine in self-defense, or even to join the Hill roads—which in turn could force most if not all other big western lines into the group. Similarly, a merger of the Pennsylvania and New York Central could force other eastern roads into their combine.

The consolidation plans of the big roads, however, cannot be selective. To keep smaller and weaker roads from importuning the ICC and so delaying the consolidation process indefinitely, the big companies would have to enlarge their aims to include all the lines in their region. In other words, the railroads themselves, given both encouragement and prodding by Washington, could push consolidation to its logical conclusion.

BIBLIOGRAPHY

An asterisk (*) preceding a reference indicates that the article or part of it has been reprinted in this book.

BOOKS AND PAMPHLETS

Alexander, E. P. American locomotives. Norton. New York. '50.

Allen, J. S. Standard time in America. National Railway Publication Co. 424 W. 33d St. New York 1. '51.

American Railway Engineering Association. Railroad field: a challenge and opportunity for engineering graduates. The Association. 59 E. Van Buren St. Chicago 5. n.d.

*Association of American Railroads. American railroads, their growth and development. The Association. Transportation Building. Washington 6, D.C. '58.

*Association of American Railroads. Day of two noons. The Association. Transportation Building. Washington 6, D.C. '59.

Association of American Railroads. Facts about featherbedding in the railway industry. The Association. Transportation Building. Washington 6, D.C. '59.

Association of American Railroads. Highways; development, use, financing. The Association. Transportation Building. Washington 6, D.C. '55.

*Association of American Railroads. Quiz on railroads and railroading. The Association. Transportation Building. Washington 6, D.C. '58.

Association of American Railroads. Railroad story. The Association. Transportation Building. Washington 6, D.C. '57.

Association of American Railroads. Railway mail story. The Association. Transportation Building. Washington 6, D.C. '57.

Barger, Harold. Transportation industries, 1889-1946; a study of output, employment and productivity. National Bureau of Economic Research. 261 Madison Ave. New York 16. '51.

Black, R. C. III. Railroads of the Confederacy. University of North Carolina Press. Chapel Hill. '52.

Botkin, B. A. and Harlow, A. F. Treasury of railroad folklore. Crown. New York. '53.

Bowman, H. W. Pioneer railroads. Fawcett Publications. New York 36. '54.

Brazeal, B. R. Brotherhood of sleeping car porters. Harper. New York. '46.

Bruce, A. W. Steam locomotive in America. Norton. New York. '52.

Buchanan, Lamont. Steel trails and iron horses. Putnam. New York. '55.

Buck, S. J. Agrarian crusade. Yale University Press. New Haven, Conn. '20.

Buck, S. J. Granger movement. Harvard University Press. Cambridge, Mass. '13.

Dearing, C. L. American highway policy. Brookings Institution. Washington, D.C. '41.

Dearing, C. L. and Owen, Wilfred. National transportation policy. Brookings Institution. Washington, D.C. '49.

Dewhurst, H. S. Railroad police. Charles C. Thomas. Springfield, Ill. '55.

Donovan, F. P. Jr. Railroad in literature. Railway and Locomotive Historical Society, Inc. Baker Library. Harvard Business School. Boston 63, Mass. '40.

Donovan, F. P. Jr. ed. Railroads of America. Kalmbach Publishing Co. 1027 N. Seventh St. Milwaukee 3, Wis. '49.

Eastern Railroad Presidents Conference. Yearbook of railroad information, 1959. The Conference. 143 Liberty St. New York 6. '59.

Ellis, C. H. British railway history. Macmillan. New York. '54.

Farrington, S. K. Jr. Railroading around the world. Coward-McCann. New York. '55.

Farrington, S. K. Jr. Railroading from the rear end. Coward-McCann. New York. '46.

Farrington, S. K. Jr. Railroading the modern way. Coward-McCann. New York. '51.

Farrington, S. K. Jr. Railroads at war. Coward-McCann. New York. '44.

Farrington, S. K. Jr. Railroads of today. Coward-McCann. New York. '49.

Forman, H. W. and Josserand, Peter. Rights of trains. Simmons-Boardman. New York. '52.

Fort, Osborn. Fun on the 5:15. Hewlett Publishing Co. South Orange, N.J. '51.

Freed, C H. Story of railroad passenger fares. The Author. Washington, D.C. '42.

Gray, C. R. Jr. Railroading in eighteen countries. Scribner. New York. '55.
    Military Railway Service, 1862-1953.

Hammell, A. L. Wm. Frederick Harnden (1813-1845), founder of the express business in America. Newcomen Society in North America. 30 Rockefeller Plaza. New York 20. '54.
    Text of address.

Haney, L. H. Congressional history of railways in the United States. 2v. Democrat Printing Co. Madison, Wis. '08, '10.

Hatch, Alden. American Express. Doubleday. Garden City, N.Y. '50.

Henry, R. S. This fascinating railroad business. Bobbs-Merrill. Indianapolis. '46.

Henry, R. S. Trains. Bobbs-Merrill. Indianapolis. '54.

Hines, W. D. War history of the American railroads. Yale University Press. New Haven, Conn. '28.

Holbrook, S. H. Age of the moguls. (Main Stream of America Series) Doubleday. Garden City, N.Y. '53.

*Holbrook, S. H. Story of the American railroads. Crown. New York. '47.

Hungerford, Edward. Wells Fargo: advancing the American frontier. Random House. New York. '49.

Husband, Joseph. Story of the Pullman car. McClurg. Chicago. '17.

Jones, H. E. Railroad wages and labor relations. Bureau of Information of the Eastern Railways. 5710 Grand Central Terminal. New York 17. '53.

Keir, R. M. March of commerce. (Pageant of America Series) Yale University Press. New Haven, Conn. '27.

Kirkland, E. C. Men, cities, and transportation. Harvard University Press. Cambridge, Mass. '48.

Laut, A. C. Romance of the rails. 2v. McBride. New York. '29; 1v. ed. Tudor Publishing Co. New York. '36.

Leonard, W. N. Railroad consolidation under the transportation act of 1920. Columbia University Press. New York. '46.

Lewis, R. G. Handbook of American railroads. Simmons-Boardman. New York. '56.

Lloyd, Roger. Fascination of railways. Macmillan. New York. '51.

Long, B. A. and Dennis, W. J. Mail by rail. Simmons-Boardman. New York. '51.

Marshall, James. Santa Fe: the railroad that built an empire. Random House. New York. '45.

Meeks, C. L. V. Railroad station. Yale University Press. New Haven, Conn. '56.

Moody, John. Railroad builders. (Chronicles of America Series) Yale University Press. New Haven, Conn. '20.

Morgan, D. P. ed. Steam's finest hour. Kalmbach Publishing Co. 1027 N. Seventh St. Milwaukee 3, Wis. '59.

Parmelee, J. H. Modern railway. Longmans. New York. '40.

Quiett, G. C. They built the west. Appleton-Century. New York. '34.

Railway Express Agency. Cavalcade of Express. The Agency. 219 E. 42d St. New York 17. '54.

Reck, F. M. Romance of American transportation. Crowell. New York. '38.

Riegel, R. E. America moves west. Holt. New York. '47.

Robertson, Archie. Slow train to yesterday. Houghton. Boston. '45.

Rose, J. R. American wartime transportation. Crowell. New York. '53.

St. Clair, Labert. Transportation since time began: land, air, water. Dodd. New York. '42.

Slichter, S. H. Union policies and industrial management. Brookings Institution. Washington, D.C. '41.

Starr, J. W. Jr. One hundred years of American railroading. Dodd. New York. '28.

Thompson, Slason. Short history of American railways, covering ten decades. Appleton. New York. '25.

Throm, E. L. Popular Mechanic's picture history of American transportation. Simon and Schuster. New York. '52.

*Van Fleet, J. A. Rail transport and the winning of wars. Association of American Railroads. Transportation Building. Washington 6, D.C. '56.

Weber, Thomas. Northern railroads in the Civil War, 1861-1865. King's Crown Press (Columbia University Press). New York. '52.

Periodicals

America. 102:392-4. Ja. 2, '60. Featherbedding on the railroads? B. L. Masse.

American Heritage. 9:56-73+. D. '57. Farewell to steam. O. O. Jensen.

American Heritage. 9:10-13+. Je. '58. Legend of Jim Hill. Stewart Holbrook.

American Magazine. 158:20-1+. Jl. '54. Riding the rails with the fast freight. E. M. Wylie.

American Magazine. 159:28-31+. Mr. '55. Around America by rail. D. H. Eddy.

American Mercury. 80:111-14. My. '55. You can't lose a freight car. J. B. Kemmerer.

*Analysts Journal. 15:29-33. F. '59. What price featherbedding? J. R. Sullivan.

Atlantic Monthly. 194:93-5. Ag. '54. Meals in motion. H. F. Ellis.
  Same abridged: Reader's Digest. 65:82-4. N. '54.

Atlantic Monthly. 200:59-62. Jl. '57. Railroads punish the passenger. J. L. Hess.

Business Week. p 120-1+. O. 8, '55. Old law breeds trouble on the rails.

Business Week. p 122-5+. F. 4, '56. Jim Hill's dream revived.

Business Week. p 48-9. My. 25, '57. Railroads' dilemma becomes a public dilemma.

Business Week. p 141+. Ja. 18, '58. Passengers; curse of railroads.

Business Week. p 148-52. Ja. 18, '58. Three railroads try three answers to commuting riddle.

Business Week. p 54-6+. N. 8, '58. Rival ways for freight to ride piggyback.

Business Week. p 106-8+. Mr. 21, '59. Long Island Railroad works its way back.

Carbuilder (Pullman-Standard) p 2-31. Mr. '55. Mainline story of Pullman-Standard.

Coronet. 26:165-8. My. '49. Anything goes by express. Norman Carlisle and Madelyn Carlisle.

*Current History. 27:7-12. Jl. '54. Railroad brotherhoods: special treatment. E. D. Wickersham.

*Economic Trends and Outlook. 4:3-4. S.-O. '59. Railroad propaganda ignores facts.

Fortune. 35:96-103+. My. '47. Mr. Young and his C & O.

Fortune. 38:122-7+. N. '48. Santa Fe: no 1 railroad.

Fortune. 39:86-90+. Ap. '49. Capture of the New Haven.

Fortune. 47:137-9+. Je. '53. Railroad-trucker brawl.

Fortune. 53:232. My. '56. Vest pocket railroad empire.

Fortune. 54:82-91+. Ag. '56. Canadian Pacific: overdue. Herbert Solow.

Fortune. 54:200. Ag. '56. How the CPR saved Canada for the Canadians.

*Fortune. 55:102-5+. Ja. '57. Great U. S. freight cartel. Gilbert Burck.

Fortune. 57:137-9+. F. '58. What hope for the railroads? E. T. Thompson.

*Fortune. 58:82-6+. Ag. '58. Plan to save the railroads. Gilbert Burck.
    Same abridged: Reader's Digest. 73:148-50+. N. '58.

*Fortune. 61:118-19+. Ja. '60. What's wrong with the railroads? P. M. Shoemaker.

Harper's Magazine. 213:81-2. S. '56. Grease my wheels. A. R. Allen.

Harper's Magazine. 214:29-33. Ap. '57. Better deal for commuters. George Alpert.

*Harper's Magazine. 217:31-6. N. '58. Unsnarling traffic on the roads, rails, and airways. J. I. Snyder, Jr.

Holiday. 22:76-7+. Jl. '57. Boyhood journey. W. D. Edmonds.

*Holiday. 27:11-22. F. '60. Trains and the mind of man. Jacques Barzun.

Mississippi Valley Historical Review. 32:171-94. S. '45. Railroad land grant legend in American history texts. R. S. Henry.

Monthly Labor Review. 81:879-81. Ag. '58. Labor-management relations under the Railway Labor Act, 1934-57.

*Nation. 187:467-71. D. 20, '58. Railroads versus the commuter. F. J. Cook.
    Reply. 188:inside cover. Ja. 10, '59. H. F. Reves.

Nation. 189:128-33. S. 12, '59. Railroad labor crisis. John Barden.

Nation's Business. 42:38-9. Ag. '54. Railroad research. D. C. Spaulding.

Nation's Business. 43:66-9. Jl. '55. Moving ahead. D. C. Spaulding.

New York Times. p F 1+. Mr. 20, '60. Railroads are focusing their attention on mergers. R. E. Bedingfield.

New York Times Magazine. p 11+. Ap. 13, '58. Railroads seek a clear track. G. A. Smathers.

*Newsweek. 46:89-94. N. 21, '55. Revolution on rails. J. A. Conway.

Newsweek. 51:78-80. Ja. 20, '58. Railroads: the track ahead.

Newsweek. 52:71-3. Ag. 11, '58. Who pays for the ride?

Newsweek. 53:82-3+. Ja. 26, '59. Late trains, hot tempers, is there any future in commuting? J. A. Conway.

Newsweek. 53:73-4. F. 23, '59. Ruffling the feathers.

*Reader's Digest. 68:181-2. F. '56. Case of the wandering freight car. W. D. Bien.

Reader's Digest. 71:147-50. D. '57. Clear track to California! 20th Century Limited and Santa Fe's Super Chief. J. D. Ratcliff.

*Reader's Digest. 72:48-53. Je. '58. Twenty hour week on the railroads. D. I. Mackie.

*Reader's Digest. 72:48-53. Je, '58. 20-hour week on the railorads. business? D. I. Mackie.

Reader's Digest. 75:76-80. N. '59. It's showdown time for feather-bedding on the railroads. Alfred Steinberg.

Reporter. 19:19-24. Ag. 7, '58. Railroads: from overlord to underdog. Robert Bendiner.
    Discussion: 19:5. S. 4, '58.

*Reporter. 21:35-7. O, 1. '59. When trains were really trains. Oliver La Farge.

Saturday Evening Post. 221:30-1+. O. 16; 30+. O. 23, '48. Errand boy number one (Railway Express Agency). A. W. Baum.

Saturday Evening Post. 229:20-1+. O. 22, '56. So you don't ride the trains any more? H. H. Martin.

Saturday Evening Post. 232:38-9+. O. 17, '59. Railroads are fighting back. Milton MacKaye.

Saturday Review. 37:29-30. O. 9, '54. Choo-choo to Broadway; show-trains, movie-trains, opera-trains.

Time. 69:94-101. Ja. 28, '57. New age of railroads.
    Same abridged: Reader's Digest. 70:80-3. My. '57.

*Time. 75:74-8. Ja. 18, '60. Those rush-hour blues.

U.S. News & World Report. 38:19-23. Ap. 8, '55. Rails vs. autos: new battle ahead.

U.S. News & World Report. 43:95-7. D. 20, '57. Story of an industry that's forced to be wasteful. B. W. Heineman.
    Same abridged with title What's wrong with the railroads? Reader's Digest. 72:32-4. Mr. '58.

U.S. News & World Report. 44:109-12. Ja. 24, '58. What railroads urge to keep from going broke.

U.S. News & World Report. 45:36-9. O. 3, '58. Dying passenger train.

U.S. News & World Report. 47:112-14. S. 28, '59. Why the trains may stop running.

U.S. News & World Report. 47:102-5. N. 9, '59. Another labor law that faces a big test: railway labor act.

U.S. News & World Report. 47:101-2. D. 21, '59. One industry that now wants compulsory arbitration.

*U.S. News & World Report. 48:100-2. F. 1, '60. "To market to market . . ." by truck on a train.

Vital Speeches of the Day. 20:731-4. S. 15, '54. First freedom: railroads have been denied the freedom to compete. B. F. Fairless.

Vital Speeches of the Day. 23:211-14. Ja. 15, '57. Pricing problem in the railroad industry. A. E. Perlman.

Vital Speeches of the Day. 23:367-71. Ap. 1, '57. Inflation and compulsory unionism. F. G. Gurley.

Vital Speeches of the Day. 24:565-8. Jl. 1, '58. Can technology solve our railroad problem? A. E. Perlman.

Vital Speeches of the Day. 25:87-90. N. 15, '58. Tide in the affairs of railroads. J. M. Symes.

Vital Speeches of the Day. 26:175-9. Ja. 1, '60. Are railroad workers "featherbedding"? G. E. Leighty.

Woman's Day. 16:62+. My. '53. Day of two noons. Stewart Holbrook.